Legal Almanac Series No. 53

LEGAL STATUS OF WOMEN

by PHILIP FRANCIS

*This Legal Almanac has been revised
by the Oceana Editorial Board*

Irving J. Sloan
General Editor

SECOND EDITION

1978 Oceana Publications, Inc.
Dobbs Ferry, New York

Library of Congress Cataloging in Publication Data

Francis, Philip
   Legal status of women.

   (Legal almanac series ; no. 53)
   Includes index.
   1. Women--Legal status, laws, etc.--United States.
I. Title
KF478.Z95C3   1978   346'.73'013   78-3469
ISBN 0-379-11115-2

© Copyright 1978 by Oceana Publications, Inc.

Manufactured in the United States of America

CONTENTS

INTRODUCTION

In the late sixties and seventies, "Women's Lib", became a household word. The phrase has come to mean many things to many people. Numerous books and articles have been written on its meaning and it is not within the scope of this book to discuss the nature and aims of this movement. Suffice it to say that one of its prime aims is or should be that women must be traced as individuals with the basic right to determine for themselves what they will do with their lives, whether it be a career in the professions or the business world, or to become a homemaker and mother.

In order to achieve this freedom and develop all their potentials, women must receive help from the law. Traditionally the courts have always regarded women as inferior to men and usually accorded them the same treatment as children, seeking to protect them from themselves and others.

Throughout the years various individual women have sought not to be protected, but to be treated as man's equal. As with the Civil Rights movement for blacks and other minorities, it has been a long and discouraging battle. Gradually, the walls of inequality are beginning to crumble. What follows is an attempt to show the status of women in the eyes of the law today.

Chapter I

MARRIAGE

Marriage and Age

The legal age for marriage is specified in each of the states. In some states, a court order authorizing marriage by persons under the statutory ages may be secured if the female is "pregnant, or has given birth to a child." The legal age for marriage without parental consent is now 18 in most, but not all, states. All applicants under age 24 are often required to present proof of age.

Marriage and Change of Name

When a woman marries, the most immediate change in her legal status is her name. The tradition that a married woman take the name of her husband is related to the early common law concept of marriage. Under that law, a woman ceased, legally, to be a person upon her marriage. She was without legal capacity. A husband and wife were regarded as one person, and that one person was the husband.

Marriage laws, however, do not require a woman to take the name of her husband. Women who retain their own names, however, have had difficulties with state laws governing licensing, voting, and registration. Some, but not all, of these laws have been changed. The Tennessee Supreme Court recently ruled that women do not have to take their husband's name when they marry.

After divorce or annulment, a wife may generally resume use of her maiden name, adopt a new name or continue to use that of her husband. This privilege has sometimes been limited "when there is a minor child or children."

Most states recognize the common law right to change one's name without having to go through legal proceedings as long as the change is not for fraudulent or illegal purposes. A name change can be effected through common usage. A better way of changing one's name is through application to a court. Fees for processing and publication of the change may be required, but if no objections are found, the court will authorize the name change. This provides for a clearer record for obtaining passports and for other purposes.

Women are not clamoring for the right to be known by their maiden names after marriage or for the right to change their names without their husbands' approvals. But in those instances where for some reason or another married women have expressed a desire to do this, the courts have uniformly rejected the effort. Despite the common law rule, which does not appear to differentiate between the rights of married men and their wives to change their names in an informal manner, no cases can be found in which the wife has been permitted to do this over the husband's objection. In addition, under many of the statutes that prescribe formal procedures for changing one's name, the right to do so has been either expressly or by implication denied to married women. No comparable restriction has been imposed upon married men. Finally, the law, once more either expressly or by implication, generally requires that a change in the husband's surname produce a corresponding change in that of his wife, but never the reverse.

Married Women's Domiciles

Marriage affects a person's legal domicile, that is, the place where one lives and to which, when absent, he or she intends to return. While this place is usually one's immediate reference, it is not unusual for domicile to be in one state and residence in another.

The areas of law in which a person's domicile may be important are numerous and varied. Domicile of a party for a decedent often determines whether a court has jurisdiction to hear and decide certain kinds of legal questions: *e.g.,* divorce suits, probate matters, and guardianship proceedings. The availability of many rights and privileges of citizenship also depend upon a person's domicile. These include the right to vote, to hold and therefore, to run for public office, to receive welfare assistance, or to qualify for free or limited tuition at state-operated institutions. Some obligations of citizenship — *e.g.,* jury duty and the taxability of personal and intangible property — are also determined by the juror's or taxpayer's domicile, respectively.

Clearly, then, the location of a person's domicile has important practical as well as legal consequences. In general, all men and unmarried adult women are free to choose their place of domicile and this they do automatically when they reside in the place where they intend to make their home. This domicile of free choice is otherwise for married women. Though exceptions exist, the general rule remains that a wife's domicile follows that of her husband's. This means that by law when a woman marries she loses her domicile and acquires that of her husband, no matter where she resides, or what she believes or intends.

This rule can create hardship. If a married woman owns personal property in state X, it may be taxed at the higher rate of state Y, her husband's domicile, although she is residing in state X with her husband's consent.

Some states, by statute, now permit a woman to have a legal domicile different from that of her husband. Wisconsin law states, for example: "Women shall have the same rights and privileges under the law as men in the . . . choice of residence. . . ." But nearly half the states

3

deny her the right to maintain a separate domicile.

Married Women and the Law of Support

Except for some states that impose a duty upon the wife to support the husband "under certain circumstances," the universal rule is that the primary obligation to provide financial support to the family rests upon the husband.

The precise legal duty of a husband to support his wife is rarely defined so long as the marriage is stable and the spouses are living together. This is because the courts refuse to intervene except in cases of marital breakdown. Thus even if a husband refuses to give his wife any money whatsoever for her own personal needs — clothing, for example — she cannot, as long as she continues to live with her husband, get a court order to compel him to provide her with reasonable support money. Her only recourse is to institute a suit for legal separation or divorce.

Married Women and Torts

The general rule of law is that if one person causes physical injury to another, as a result of the first person's negligence or willful misconduct, the injured person has a legal cause of action to obtain redress from the person who caused the injury. At one time under the common law, though a married woman was theoretically liable for the injuries she inflicted in this manner, that liability was of limited significance since the law attributed her misconduct to her husband. Today, the wife's immunity from suit for tort damages and the corresponding imputed liability of the husband has almost everywhere been abrogated by statute or judicial decision.

Husbands and wives under the common law were absolutely prohibited from suing each other, whatever the circumstances, including intentional serious injury.

4

Under the common law a husband and wife were regarded in law as one person so that a suit between them would in reality have been a suit by one individual against himself.

In some states spouses may now sue one another for willful infliction of injury, but most states continue to deny husband and wife the right to sue one another for negligently inflicted injuries. Most negligent injuries result from automobile accidents or other activities covered by insurance. Since it is feared that if suits are permitted between spouses for accidental injuries, too many fraudulent claims will be filed, such tort actions are generally prohibited. It is argued that husbands and wives would take advantage of insurance companies. But there are a growing number of states that now allow injury suits between spouses.

When a person is physically injured, he or she may not be the only one to suffer harm as a result of those injuries. The victim who has actually been injured may be so related to another party who has a legal right that certain attributes of the injured person remain unimpaired. This right is a relational interest. Under the law, husbands and wives have such an interest in one another. A husband or a wife may sue a third person for "loss of consortium." Loss of consortium is the loss of "conjugal" rights to enjoy a spouse's physical, sexual, and psychological well-being. If a wife or husband is injured so that one may not enjoy his or her conjugal rights, twenty-eight states and the District of Columbia permit the other spouse to bring suit for loss of consortium; sixteen permit only the husband to sue a third party for his loss. Seven states (Connecticut, Louisiana, Massachusetts, North Carolina, Rhode Island, Utah, and Virginia) have all abolished the right of either spouse to bring a lawsuit on the ground of loss of consortium.

Married Women as Witness At Trial of Husband

A husband and wife relationship presupposes a

5

privilege of uninhibited communication, without which they would presumably confide in each other only at their peril. Married couples are viewed like parties in a confidential relationship between attorney-client, doctor-patient, and priest-confessor. Such parties are not generally allowed to testify about their communications with each other where one of the parties is on trial.

However, the statutes vary on husband and wife testimonial privilege. Some hold that the privilege is personal to the witness only, and if that witness *wants* to testify for or against the spouse, the spouse cannot object. Other statutes hold that the witness may only testify against the spouse with the spouse's consent. Generally, a husband or wife need not testify against his or her spouse unless he or she wants to do so. In a criminal trial, however, if the witness desires to testify and the other spouse has given consent, then the witness must do so as if she or he were not married.

Chapter II

ABORTION RIGHTS AND WOMEN

In 1973 the United States Supreme Court rendered two decisions which resulted in making the abortion laws of nearly every state in the country either entirely or partially unconstitutional. The two companion cases were *Roe v. Wade* and *Doe v. Bolton*. The first case ruled that the Fourteenth Amendment guarantees the "right of privacy," which includes a woman's decision to seek an abortion. Thus any state law that permits abortion *only* to save the life of the mother is unconstitutional. The second case held unconstitutional those portions of the Georgia abortion statute that required abortion to be performed in specially credited hospitals, or be approved by a hospital abortion committee, or be concurred in by two doctors other than the woman's physician. This ruling also prohibited state residence requirements for women who want abortions.

Only New York had a law that met the Supreme Court's standards. Nine other states: Alaska, Georgia, Hawaii, Idaho, Indiana, Montana, North Carolina, Tennessee, and Washington — now have laws that place no over-all restrictions on a woman's right to have an abortion.

In *Alaska* an abortion is legal at any time before the fetus is viable. An unmarried woman under 18 must have the consent of parents or guardian. But this latter requirement may be unconstitutional under the *Roe v. Wade* case. The operation must be performed by a licensed physician in a hospital or other approved faculty.

There is a thirty day residence requirement which may also be unconstitutional.

In *Georgia* an abortion is legal during the first or second trimester of pregnancy if the physician considers it necessary based on his clinical judgment. After the first trimester the operation must be performed in a licensed hospital. After the second trimester, abortion may be performed only to save the mother's life or health. Two physicians must certify that it is necessary and it must be approved by a committee of the hospital's medical staff. There is a state residency requirement which is unconstitutional.

In *Hawaii* an abortion is legal at any time before the fetus is viable. The operation must be performed by a licensed physician in a licensed hospital. This hospital requirement is unconstitutional for the first trimester of pregnancy. There is an unconstitutional ninety day residence requirement.

In *Idaho* an abortion is legal during the first or second trimester (about the first twenty-five weeks of pregnancy) if the physician, after consulting with the woman, determines it is appropriate in consideration of a number of highly restrictive factors. After the fetus becomes viable, abortion may be performed only to save the life of the mother or if, on birth, the fetus would be unable to survive. No residence requirement exists.

In *Indiana* an abortion is legal during the first trimester of pregnancy if the woman consents and the operation is performed by a physician in a hospital or licensed facility. Again, the hospital requirement for the first trimester of pregnancy is unconstitutional. During the second trimester, the abortion must be performed in a hospital. An unmarried woman under 18 must have the consent of parents or guardian unless the abortion is necessary to save her life. After the fetus is viable, abortion may be performed only to save the mother's life or physical health, and the attending physician must certify in writing that it is necessary. No residence requirement exists.

8

In *Montana* an abortion is legal during the first three months of pregnancy if the woman gives her written, "informed" consent. A married woman must have the consent of her husband; an unmarried minor must have the consent of parents or guardian. The operation must be performed by a licensed physician. After the first three months, the operation must be performed in a licensed hospital. After the fetus is viable, abortion may be performed only to save the mother's life, and the attending physician must certify in writing that it is necessary, with concurrence from two other physicians. No residence requirement exists.

In *New York* an abortion is legal during the first twenty-four weeks of pregnancy. Either a licensed physician may perform the abortion or the woman herself may induce a miscarriage on the advice of a physician. After the first twenty-four weeks, abortion may be performed only if a licensed physician believes it is necessary. No residence requirement exists.

In *North Carolina* an abortion is legal during the first twenty weeks of pregnancy. The operation must be performed by a licensed physician in a licensed hospital. The hospital requirement is unconstitutional for the first trimester of pregnancy. After the first twenty weeks, abortion may be performed only if it is necessary to save the mother's life. There is a thirty day residence requirement which is unconstitutional.

In *Tennessee* an abortion is legal during the first three months of pregnancy if a licensed physician considers it necessary and the woman gives her written consent. The operation must be performed by a licensed physician. After the first three months but before the fetus is viable, the operation must be performed in a licensed hospital. After the fetus is viable, abortion may be performed only to save the mother's life or health. The woman must be a resident of the state, an unconstitutional requirement.

In *Washington* an abortion is legal during the first four months of pregnancy if the woman gives her consent. A married woman must have the consent of her husband; an unmarried minor must have the consent of parents or guardian. The operation must be performed by a licensed physician in an accredited hospital or approved facility unless the physician determines pregnancy must be terminated immediately; in that case it may be performed elsewhere. The hospital requirement for the first trimester of pregnancy is unconstitutional. A three-month residence requirement is unconstitutional.

Chapter III

CONTRACTS AND DEBTS

The Right to make Contracts

Under common law, the legal existence of the wife was merged into that of her husband. In general, therefore, the contracts of a married woman were void. Today, in every state, a married woman has had restored to her by statute many of the contractual powers that she lost under common-law rule, particularly in regard to property set apart to her as her separate legal estate.

New York State is typical of the completely broad base of women's contractual rights established by statute. In New York, a married woman may make contracts regarding property with any person including her husband, and she will be liable on those contracts as if she were unmarried. She has a right to contract for insurance on her husband's life. A husband or wife, however, cannot contract to alter or dissolve the marriage or to relieve the husband from his responsibility for support. A contract by a married woman does not bind her husband or his property, and a judgment for or against a married woman may be rendered or enforced as if she were unmarried.

Against the background of these general statements, it is useful to explore specific areas of contractual relationships:

CONTRACTS BETWEEN HUSBAND AND WIFE: Husband and wife may contract freely with each other regarding both real and personal property in 18 states. They are:

11

Arkansas, Colorado, Connecticut, Delaware, Florida, Idaho, Maryland, Michigan, Missouri, Nebraska, New Hampshire, New Jersey, New York, North Dakota, Pennsylvania, South Carolina, Utah, Wisconsin.

In 7 states, transactions between husband and wife are subject to the general rules that control the actions of persons occupying confidential relations with each other. They are:

California, Montana, Nevada, New Mexico, Ohio, Oklahoma, South Dakota.

In 5 states, there is a requirement that any transfer of personal property between the spouses must be by written instrument, and in some instances, acknowledged and filed for record. These states are:

Illinois, Kentucky, Mississippi, North Carolina, West Virginia.

Contracts between husband and wife are apparently prohibited in Massachusetts and Vermont, and restricted as to specifics in Iowa, Main, Minnesota and Oregon. The following states appear to make no statutory provision with reference to the right of husband and wife to contract with each other. They are:

Alabama, Arizona, District of Columbia, Indiana, Kansas, Louisiana, Tennessee, Texas, Virginia, Washington, Wyoming.

CONVEYANCE OF REAL PROPERTY: In 25 states, the wife may convey her real property as if she were unmarried. They are:

Arizona, Arkansas, California, Colorado, Connecticut, District of Columbia, Georgia, Idaho, Louisiana, Michigan, Mississippi, Montana, Nebraska, Nevada, New Mexico, New York, North Dakota, Oklahoma, South Carolina, South Dakota, Tennessee, Utah, Washington, Wisconsin, Wyoming.

In 15 states, a married woman's sole deed or conveyance transfers absolutely her rights and the rights of her repre-

12

sentatives in her real estate, but has no effect on the husband's interest in her lands, unless he joins in the deed or conveyance. These states are:

Delaware, Illinois, Iowa, Kansas, Maine, Maryland Massachusetts, Minnesota, Missouri, New Hampshire, New Jersey, Oregon, Rhode Island, Virginia, West Virginia.

In 8 states, the husband must join with the wife in order to make a valid conveyance. These are:

Alabama, Florida, Indiana, Kentucky, North Carolina, Ohio, Pennsylvania, Texas.

TRANSFERS OF PERSONAL PROPERTY: In all jurisdictions except Georgia and Texas, a married woman may transfer her personal property to third persons as if she were unmarried. In Georgia, a married woman may not bind her separate estate by any contract of suretyship nor by any assumption of the debts of her husband. In North Carolina, contracts affecting personal property of the wife for more than three years must be in writing. In Texas, a wife cannot make a valid transfer of stocks and bonds owned by her without the joint signature of her husband.

Engaging in Business, Earnings, Wage Assignments

The right to enter into contracts suggests, as well, the right of a married woman to engage in her own separate business. In most states, as a result of statutory enactment, a married woman may engage in an independent business, using her own funds and acting on her own liability, without interference from her husband or others claiming through him. In some states—California, Florida, Nevada, Pennsylvania and Texas—statutes require a formal procedure on the part of a married woman who desires to engage in a separate business. This usually takes the form of a petition to the court of the county in which she resides showing why the common law disability should be removed. These technical requirements, however, are more honored in the breach than in the enforcement.

It follows from the right to engage in separate business

that neither spouse is liable for the separate debts of the other. Since a wife's earnings from her separate business are a part of her separate estate, these earnings are not liable for her husband's debts. Massachusetts provides, however, that a married woman, to protect her business from her husband's creditors, must record in the town where the business is conducted a separate business certificate. In Arkansas, California, Idaho, Montana, Nevada, Oklahoma, and South Dakota, statutes permit a married woman to place on public record a list of her separate personal property, from whatever source derived, in order that her rights of ownership may be protected from her husband's creditors. California and Nevada limit the amount of the husband's investment in his wife's business to $500, and in Nevada, the wife may lose the protection of the statute if her husband participates in the management of her business.

By the same reasoning, a husband is not liable for the debts of his wife arising out of her separate business. In Louisiana, the husband may become liable if the profits from the wife's business become community property. And in Massachusetts, if the wife has not filed her "separate business certificate," the husband may be found liable for her business debts.

EARNINGS FROM THIRD PERSONS: In the 9 community property states—Arizona, California, Hawaii, Idaho, Louisiana, Nevada, New Mexico, Texas, Washington—the earnings of a wife from third persons for personal services rendered outside the home become community property. Except in Idaho and Washington, the husband has the control and management of the wife's earnings along with other community property. In California, she may control community property money earned by her until it is commingled with other community property. In Nevada, she may control her earnings when they are used for the support of the family. In states where the husband manages his wife's earnings as part of the community property, he sues alone or, as in Arizona, joins his wife in the suit. It should be noted, however, that a husband cannot dispose of the community property with intent to defraud his wife. And the earnings of a wife living separate and apart from her husband are her separate property.

In all of the other states, statutes or court decisions operate to set apart for a wife as her separate property her earnings from third persons for personal services. These are free from her husband and his creditors, irrespective of his consent. These states give the wife control and management of her separate earnings, as well as the right to recover them in her own right. In Iowa, North Carolina and Pennsylvania, a wife may recover from her husband for services rendered to him beyond the scope of family and household duties, when a definite agreement or intention between them can be established.

WAGE ASSIGNMENTS: Assignment of wages—the promise of a wage earnier to pay a portion or all of his earnings to a creditor or other person—is restricted by law in more than half the states. In 16 of the states, the written assent of the wage earner's spouse is necessary to make the assignment valid. The states are:

Arizona, California, Colorado, Georgia, Idaho, Illinois, Iowa, Maryland, Michigan, Nebraska, Oklahoma, Rhode Island, Utah, Vermont, Virginia, West Virginia.

In 9 states, the wife's assent is required to an assignment of wages by the husband, but there is no requirement of the husband's assent to assignment of wages by the wife. These are:

Arkansas, Indiana, Louisiana, Massachusetts, Minnesota, Montana, Texas, Wisconsin, Wyoming.

New Mexico requires that the wage assignment of a married man must be recorded to be valid.

Exemption of Property from Seizure for Debt

All states have enacted some legislation granting exemptions of specified real and personal property from siezure and sale to satisfy the owner's personal debts.

WAGES: Garnishment is the procedure by which a creditor may reach the wages of a debtor. It is to be distinguished from the situation where a debtor voluntarily makes an assignment of his wages to a creditor.

The amount of wages held exempt from garnishment varies considerably among the states. In 20 states, wages are exempt if the money is necessary for family support. The exemptions range from all the debtor's earnings (unless the debt was contracted for necessaries or for personal services rendered by an employee of the debtor) in California, to $20 a week in Washington. The states are:

> Arizona, California, Colorado, District of Columbia, Idaho, Illinois, Kansas, Michigan, Minnesota, Mississippi, Missouri Nebraska, North Carolina, North Dakota, Oregon, South Carolina, Utah, Washington, Wisconsin, Wyoming.

In an additional 25 states, a portion of wages or earnings of a debtor, regardless of family status, is exempt. Such exemptions vary from a flat $15 a week in Connecticut to all wages for a 90-day period in Iowa. The states are:

> Alabama, Connecticut, Delaware, Florida, Indiana, Iowa, Kentucky, Louisiana, Maine, Maryland, Massachusetts, Montana, Nevada, New Jersey New Mexico, New York, Ohio, Oklahoma, Rhode Island, Tennessee, Texas, Vermont, Virginia, West Virginia.

The states of Arkansas, Georgia, New Hampshire, Pennsylvania and South Dakota have no specific provision for wage exemption.

PERSONAL PROPERTY: In 7 states, any personal property up to a certain value is exempt from seizure for debt. In the calculation of this basic exemption, wages, earnings and insurance are generally excluded. The value of property so exempt ranges from $200 in West Virginia to $2,000 in Louisiana. The states are:

> Florida, Indiana, Louisiana, Michigan, North Carolina, South Carolina, West Virginia.

In 5 additional states—Alabama, Arkansas, Ohio, South

16

Dakota and Virginia—a debtor is permitted to claim exemption of property up to a certain value, in addition to specified articles of classes of personal property.

The following categories of "personal property" are variously specifically covered:

Life Insurance—Except in 10 states—Arkansas, California, Colorado, Delaware, Georgia, Indiana, Massachusetts, Nebraska, Rhode Island and Virginia—all or a specified part of the proceeds of life insurance taken out for the benefit of the wife on the life of her husband is exempt from seizure by creditors. A fewer number of states have enacted a corresponding provision for the benefit of the husband as to insurance on the life of his wife.

Household goods—Except for those states that set a flat value on personal property exempt from seizure for debt—Florida, Indiana, Louisiana, Michigan, North Carolina, South Carolina and West Virginia—all states provide for some exemption of household furniture and furnishings in use by the debtor and his family. The amount of the exemption varies from state to state.

Wearing apparel—Wearing apparel of a debtor and his family is specifically exempt in 39 states, the majority of which exempt all such property, regardless of value. The states are:

Alabama, Arizona, Arkansas, California, Colorado, Connecticut, Delaware, District of Columbia, Georgia, Idaho, Illinois, Iowa, Kansas, Kentucky, Maine, Maryland, Massachusetts, Minnesota, Mississippi, Missouri, Montana, Nebraska, Nevada, New Hampshire, New Jersey, New Mexico, New York, North Dakota, Ohio, Oregon, Pennsylvania, Rhode Island, South Dakota, Texas, Vermont, Virginia, Washington, Wisconsin, Wyoming.

Family provisions—Food and other provisions necessary for family support are statutorily exempt in 29 states. Massachusetts and Ohio place a $50 value on such provisions, while Wyoming exempts $500 of family provisions and household equipment. The states are:

Arizona, California, Colorado, Connecticut, District of Columbia, Georgia, Idaho, Iowa, Kansas, Louisiana, Massachusetts, Minnesota, Mississippi, Missouri, Montana, Nebraska, Nevada, New York, North Dakota, Ohio, Oklahoma, Oregon, South Dakota, Texas, Utah, Vermont, Virginia, Wisconsin, Wyoming.

Tools of trade—Specific exemption of a debtor's trade tools or his farm or professional equipment is made in 38 states. Statutes governing exemption of such equipment include professional libraries, office furniture, musical instruments and sewing machines. Generally, all such equipment is exempt. However, Wisconsin and Ohio set a $200 value and Oregon a $400 value. New Jersey exempts such property only if there are other goods sufficient for levy. The states are:

Arizona, California, Colorado, Connecticut, Delaware, District of Columbia, Georgia, Idaho, Iowa, Kansas, Kentucky, Maine, Maryland, Massachusetts, Michigan, Minnesota, Mississippi, Missouri, Montana, Nebraska, Nevada, New Jersey, New Mexico, New York, North Dakota, Ohio, Oklahoma, Oregon, South Dakota, Tennessee, Texas, Utah, Vermont, Virginia, Washington, West Virginia, Wisconsin, Wyoming.

In the application of these statutory exemptions, the statutes generally do not make distinctions between men and women. The emphasis in 26 states is placed on "head of a family," who is given a larger exemption than single person. In the other jurisdictions, no differentiation is made. Those states which favor the "head of a family," are:

Arkansas, Colorado, Delaware, District of Columbia, Florida Georgia, Illinois, Iowa, Kansas, Kentucky, Louisiana, Mississippi, Missouri, Nebraska, New Jersey, New Mexico, North Dakota, Ohio, Oklahoma, South Carolina, South Dakota, Tennessee, Texas, Virginia, Wisconsin, Wyoming.

REAL PROPERTY: With the exception of Delaware, District of Columbia, Maryland, Pennsylvania, and Rhode Island, all states have enacted "Homestead Laws" which have as their purpose the safeguarding of the family against debtors. These laws include those exempting the home from seizure for debt, restricting the sale or other conveyance without the assent of both husband and wife, and permitting a surviving spouse to continue to occupy the family home following the death of his or her mate. Where "homestead" is specifically defined, it generally includes the home occupied by the family plus outbuildings and, in rural areas, a specified acreage.

Persons entitled to exemption—30 states declare that the head of a family, i.e. a person on whom others are dependent for support, is entitled to a homestead exemption from seizure for debt by creditors. The states are:

Arizona, Arkansas, Georgia, Idaho, Illinois, Iowa, Kansas, Kentucky, Louisiana, Massachusetts, Mississippi, Missouri, Montana, Nebraska, Nevada, New Jersey, New Mexico, New York, North Dakota, Ohio, Oklahoma, Oregon, South Carolina, South Dakota, Tennessee, Texas, Utah, Washington, West Virginia, Wyoming.

In 11 states, the exemption is accorded to property owners regardless of "head of family" status. These are:

Alabama, Colorado, Connecticut, Florida, Maine, Michigan, New Hampshire, North Carolina, Vermont, Virginia, Wisconsin.

California and Idaho differentiate between heads of families and property owners, giving a higher exemption to the former. Minnesota declares that a "husband or wife" is entitled to the statutory exemption. A few states specifically provide that if a husband fails to claim the homestead exemption, the wife may do so.

To illustrate the various property exemptions—both personal and real property—as provided in a specific jurisdiction, the reader is furnished the following summary of the law in New York State.

The following personal proprety owned by a householder is exempt from seizure for debt: (a) Wearing apparel; (b) household furniture, tableware, cooking utensils, refrigerators, stove and fuel and family provisions for

60 days; (c) sewing machine; (d) family Bible, pictures and books; (e) radio; (f) domestic animals and feed; (g) wedding ring and watch not evceeding $35 in value; (h) tools and implements, including furniture and library not exceeding in value $600, necessary to carry on debtor's profession or vocation; and (i) church pew. These articles are not exempt from execution for a debt owed for work performed by a domestic laborer or mechanic, or for the purchase price (Civ. Prac. Act, sec. 665).

Where the judgment debtor is a woman, whether or not she is a householder, she is entitled to the same exemptions as a householder (Civ. Prac. Act, sec. 665-a).

Exempt presonal property owned by a man who is not a householder includes: (a) Church pew; (b) wearing apparel; (c) wedding ring; (d) watch not exceeding $35 in value; and (e) working tools and implements including furniture and library not exceeding in value $400 necessary for the debtor's profession or vocation. These items are not exempt from execution for money owed a laborer, mechanic, or domestic; or for purchase price (Civ. Prac. Act, sec. 666).

The earnings of a judgment debtor for his personal services rendered within 60 days before the action was begun, are exempt where it is established satisfactorily that those earnings are necessary for the use of him and his famliy if dependent upon him (Civ. Prac. Act, sec. 792).

The amount collectible under a wage assignment relating to any indebtedness aggregating less than $1,000 may not exceed 10 percent of the assigner's future wages in any month (Pers. Prop., sec. 48-a). No portion of the assigner's future earnings may be withheld by reason of any wage assignment unless such earnings amount to at least $30 a week, if the assigner is employed in a city of 250,000 or more population, or $25 a week if employed elsewhere (Pers. Prop., sec. 48-b).

Where judgment has been recovered and execution issued, ajudgment debtor may abbly to the court for an exemption of $30 a week if he resides in a city of 250,00C or more population, or $25 a week in other places (Civ. Prac. Act, sec. 684).

Life insurance proceeds payable to or for the benefit of a married woman are exempt from claim of creditors or representatives of her husband or her own creditors (Ins., sec. 166).

A plot of land with one or more buildings not exceeding in value $1,000, owned and occupied as a residence by a householder, designated as a homestead, is exempt from sale by execution issued upon a judgment unless the debt was contracted before the designation of the property or for the purchase money. No property is exempt from sale for nonpayment of taxes (Civ. Prac. Act, sec. 671). In order to designate property as a homestead, a conveyance stating that it is designed to be held as a homestead must be recorded (Civ. Prac. Act, sec. 672). A woman may designate a homestead in the same manner as a male householder (Civ. Prac. Act, sec. 673).

If the homestead exceeds $1,000 in value the lien against the judgment debtor attaches to the surplus as if the property had not been designated as an exempt homestead (Civ. Prac. Act, sec. 676).

A homestead exemption continues after the death of the owner for the benefit of the surviving spouse and children until the youngest child reaches the age of majority and until the death of the surviving spouse. The exemption lapses if the property ceases to be occupied as a residence by the person for whose benefit it continued (Civ. Prac. Act, sec. 674).

Credit and Women

For some time now women's groups have been denouncing credit policies which have been practiced throughout the nation.

Women, particularly married and divorced women, have been discriminated against solely on the basis of their sex. Most of their applications for loans had to be countersigned by another person (usually a male). Obtaining a mortgage, for most women was almost impossible, even if they possessed a relatively high paying job. Particularly disheartening was the difficulty that working married couples experienced in obtaining a mortgage. Lending institutions would not consider the combined salary of the husband and wife in determining eligibility for a mortgage. Unless the wife was over child bearing age, or could furnish proof of a hysterectomy, usually only the husband's salary was considered.

For the past several years, some banks and federal lending companies have begun to discontinue this type of discrimination. Several states, such as New York, began to pass legislation outlawing discriminatory credit practices.

Perhaps the greatest impetus will come from the "Equal Credit Opportunity Act", effective October 1975. That Congress has become aware of the problem is clear from the statement of purpose of the act, which reads as follows:

"That Congress finds that there is a need to insure that the various financial institutions and other firms engaged in the extensions of credit exercise their responsibility to make credit available with fairness, impartiality, and without discrimination on the basis of sex or marital status. Economic stabilization would be enhanced and competition among the various financial institutions and other firms engaged in the extension of credit would be strengthened by an absence of discrimination on the basis of sex or marital status, as well as by the informed use of credit which Congress has heretofore sought to promote. It is the purpose of this Act to require that financial institutions and other firms engaged in the extension of credit make that credit equally available to all creditworthy customers without regard to sex or marital status."

Under the act it is unlawful for any creditor to discriminate against any applicant on the basis of sex or marital status with respect to any aspect of a credit transaction. A creditor may inquire into the marital status only for the purpose of ascertaining the creditor's rights and remedies with respect to any aspect of the transaction.

Any creditor who fails to comply with the provisions of this action is subject to a civil suit, and liable for the amount of damages actually sustained as a result of the credit rejection. If the aggrieved applicant brings the suit individually, punitive damages may also be granted by the court in an amount not greater than $10,000.

As of this writing, there have been no reported cases relating to this relatively new law.

Chapter IV

PROPERTY RIGHTS AND INHERITANCE

Interests in Real and Personal Property

Under common law, all of a wife's personal property in her possession at the time of the marriage vested absolutely in her husband. Intangibles—such as bonds, corporate stocks, claims for damage, etc.—belonging to the woman at the time of the marriage vested in the husband merely by the excercise of some act of ownership over them. While the husband did not acquire ownership of his wife's realty upon marriage, he did have a freehold interest in all lands owned by her with the right to possession and control during the marriage.

Under statutory law, however, a wife now retains the ownership of all property, both real and personal belonging to her at the time of marriage, and statutes have been enacted in all states giving her the right to acquire property which she may hold as her separate estate. As previously noted, it is generally true that neither the separate property of a married woman nor its income or profit becomes subject to the husband's debts. As a rule, neither spouse is liable for the debts of the other incurred before marriage, and each spouse is liable for his or her own debts contracted before or after marriage.

In the area of property acquired by joint efforts of husband and wife, the applicable legal picture is somewhat more complicated. In the non-community property states, property acquired by the husband and wife during marriage is generally under the management and control of the husband. However, the states have imposed statutory restrictions on disposition and use of certain types of property.

All states recognize joint ownership of both real and personal property. In fact, this system is widely used by husbands and wives with respect to bank accounts, securities, furniture, automobile and real property ownership since it protects the interests of the other if one of the spouses dies or becomes legally incapacitated. Because the legal implications are very different, it is worthwhile to explore the various methods of joint ownership.

TENANCY BY THE ENTIRETY: This was the common law form of joint ownership, which still prevails in Arkansas, Delaware, Massachusetts, Missouri, Vermont and Wyoming. The estate can be terminated or mortgaged during marriage only by the joint action of the husband and wife. Such an estate is liable for the joint debts of husband and wife only, but the rights of survivorship of the husband and his right to possession and enjoyment of the profits of land held by the entirety are liable for his debts. At the death of either, the property belongs outright to the surviving spouse.

In an additional 11 states, a joint ownership will be presumed to be by the entirety, unless the deed or instrument establishing the estate clearly expresses a contrary intention. These states are:

District of Columbia, Florida, Indiana, Maryland, Michigan, New Jersey, New York, North Carolina, Oregon, Pennsylvania, Tennessee.

TENANCY IN COMMON: This is an interest in land by two or more persons who hold such interest by separate and distinct titles, each party being entitled to an undivided interest in the property. Each party may dispose of his interest without the assent of the other tenants, and at death, the interest of such a party descends to his heirs or assigns, not to the surviving tenants. In Kentucky, Mississippi, Rhode Island, Utah and Virginia, a conveyance to husband and wife is presumed to create a tenancy in common, unless a contrary intention to create either a tenancy by entirety or a joint tenancy is clearly expressed. In 15 additional states, a tenancy in common is presumed unless an intent to create a joint tenancy is shown. These states are:

Alabama, Colorado, Connecticut, Iowa, Kansas, Maine, Minnesota, Montana, Nebraska, New Hampshire, North Dakota, Oklahoma, South Carolina, South Dakota, West Virginia.

Georgia, Illinois and Ohio rule that a husband and wife may hold property only as tenants in common.

JOINT TENANCY: This is an interest in land held by several persons. Each has the right to dispose of his interest without the assent of the others. On the death of one of the parties in interest, the survivor or survivors succeed to the estate. Only in Wisconsin are husband and wife limited to joint tenancy as the method by which they may hold real property.

In 9 states, there exists a system of property ownership known as "community property." The states are:

Arizona, California, Hawaii, Idaho, Louisiana, Nevada, New Mexico, Texas, Washington.

Under this system of law, the property acquired by the husband and wife, or by either of them during the marriage, otherwise than by ways which clearly suggest "separate property," is community property. The general rule in community property states is that the husband is the head of the "community" and the duty is his to manage the property for the benefit of his wife and family. Usually, as long as the husband is capable of managing the community, the wife has no power of control over it and, acting alone, cannot contract debts chargeable against it. However, in Arizona, California, Hawaii, Idaho, New Mexico and Washington, the wife must join in a conveyance of real property which is part of the community. In Louisiana, the husband may convey real property alone unless it is in the wife's name, in which case, she must

25

give her written consent. In Nevada, the wife must join in a conveyance of the homestead. In Texas, the husband has sole power of disposition of both real and personal property.

Although briefly discussed in connection with property protected against creditors, the concept of the "homestead" has additional important implications for both husband and wife. The husband is usually given the right to select the homestead, although the wife may be so empowered where the husband fails to do so. It may be selected from the property of either spouse or from the common property of the marriage. After the homestead has been declared, 32 states require that consent of both husband and wife is required before it can be validly conveyed or sold, notwithstanding that ownership may be in one spouse. The states are:

> Alabama, Arizona, Arkansas, California, Colorado, Hawaii, Idaho, Illinois, Iowa, Kansas, Kentucky, Michigan, Minnesota, Mississippi, Montana, Nebraska, Nevada, New Hampshire, New Jersey, New Mexico, North Carolina, North Dakota, Ohio, Oklahoma, South Carolina, Tennessee, Texas, Utah, Vermont, Washington, Wyoming.

In California, Hawaii, Idaho, Nevada and Washington, there are formal procedures set out for abandonment of the family homestead, and Iowa provides that if the owner of a homestead changes its limits or vacates it, such action does not affect the rights of the owner's spouse or children if it was done without his or her concurrence.

The surviving spouse has a vested interest in the homestead on the death of the husband or wife. The interest may consist of absolute ownership (California, Colorado, Kansas, Vermont, Wyoming) or a life interest (Connecticut, Illinois, Nebraska, New Hampshire, North Dakota, Oklahoma, South Dakota, Texas). In all cases, the interest is protected from creditors up to the amount set forth by statute (See Chart which follows). In community property states, where a homestead was not selected before the death of a spouse, the court will usually set aside a "probate homestead" for the benefit of the surviving husband or wife.

In addition to the protection against creditors, the survivor retains the right of homestead even though the decedent died with a Will which attempted to dispose of it. In such an instance the surviving spouse can elect against the Will and so take the homestead.

In states where the surviving spouse is entitled to dower or curtesy, the right of homestead is sometimes considered a part of the dower or curtesy interest, while in other states where the spouse takes as heir under the laws of inheritance, the homestead is in addition to any other share allowed by statute

The following chart illustrates the limit of value and area of the homestead in the several states. A few of our states, such as Florida and Kansas, do not place a limit on the value of the homestead, although the acreage may be limited. In Kansas the statute defines a homestead as 160 acres without, or of one acre lying within, the limits of an incorporated city which is used as a residence at the time of one spouse's death (Gen. Stat. §59-401).

Homestead

State	Limit of Value	Limit of Area
ALABAMA	$6,000	160 acres
ARIZONA	$4,000	None
ARKANSAS	$2,500	1 acre in city, town or village; 100 acres elsewhere
CALIFORNIA	$7,500	None
COLORADO	$5,000	None
CONNECTICUT	$1,000	None
DELAWARE	No law	—
DISTRICT OF COLUMBIA	No law	—
FLORIDA	None	½ acre in city or town; 160 acres elsewhere
GEORGIA	$500	50 acres outside of town or city
IDAHO	$5,000	None
ILLINOIS	$1,000	None
INDIANA	No law	—

State	Limit of Value	Limit of Area
IOWA	$500	½ acre in city or town; 40 acres elsewhere
KANSAS	None	1 acre in city or town; 60 acres elsewhere
KENTUCKY	$1,000	None
LOUISIANA	$4,000	160 acres
MAINE	$1,000	None
MARYLAND	No law	—
MASSACHUSETTS	$4,000	None
MICHIGAN	$2,500	1 lot in city, town or village; 40 acres elsewhere
MINNESOTA	None	⅓ acre in city, village or borough over 5,000 population; ½ acre if less than 5,000 population; 80 acres elsewhere
MISSISSIPPI	$5,000	160 acres
MISSOURI	$1,500 in country $3,000 in city	160 acres in country; 30 sq. rods to 5 acres in city (depending on population)
MONTANA	$2,500	¼ acre in city or town; 320 acres of agricultural land
NEBRASKA	$2,000	2 lots in city or village; 160 acres in country
NEVADA	$10,000	None
NEW HAMPSHIRE	$1,000	None
NEW JERSEY	$1,000	None
NEW MEXICO	$1,000	None
NEW YORK	$1,000	None
NORTH CAROLINA	$1,000	None
NORTH DAKOTA	$25,000 in town No limit in country.	2 acres in town; 160 acres in country
OHIO	$1,000	None
OKLAHOMA	$5,000	160 acres if rural
OREGON	$5,000	1 block in city; 160 acres elsewhere
PENNSYLVANIA	No law	—
RHODE ISLAND	No law	—
SOUTH CAROLINA	$1,000	None

State	Limit of Value	Limit of Area
SOUTH DAKOTA	$5,000	1 acre in town; 160 acres in country
TENNESSEE	$1,000	None
TEXAS	$5,000	200 acres in country
UTAH	$2,000 plus $750 for wife and $300 for each other member	None
VERMONT	$1,000	None
VIRGINIA	$2,000	None
WASHINGTON	$6,000	None
WEST VIRGINIA	$1,000	None
WISCONSIN	$5,000	40 acres of agricultural land; ¼ acre otherwise
WYOMING	$2,500	None

Rights Of Surviving Spouse

At common law the surviving spouse had a right of dower or curtesy in the real property of the deceased spouse. The surviving wife's dower right consisted of a one-third interest for life in all the real property owned by the husband during his life. Curtesy was the right of the husband to life estate in all of the deceased wife's real property. The life estate which is taken consists of the use and enjoyment of real property for the duration of the recipient's life; including all rents and profits which are derived from the land. This interest can usually be sold or assigned subject always to termination on the death of the original recipient.

Dower and curtesy attach to any property which the spouse owned at any time during the marriage, whether or not such property was conveyed by deed. The right is usually barred, however, where both husband and wife join in a conveyance of the property.

DOWER: Under our present statutes many variations of the common law right of dower exist. In some states the right has been completely abolished, while in others statutory substitutions or modification have been enacted. Certain requirements are necessary for a widow to be entitled to dower namely: (1) Lawful marriage; (2) The husband was possessed of an estate of inheritance in property, i.e., he owned a real property interest; and (3) The wife must survive the husband. Although the requirements are derived from common law they have usually been incorporated in the statutes of those states which have retained the dower right.

Under certain circumstances the right of dower may be defeated. The wife can release her right by joining in the conveyance of the property by her husband or by a property settlement between the husband and wife. The right of dower is usually barred where the wife abandons her husband without just cause or is divorced because of her adultery or other misconduct. Condemnation proceedings, which is the lawful taking of property by the state or local government, usually bars dower. The dower right always terminates on the death of the widow.

CURTESY: The common law right of curtesy has been abolished either expressly or impliedly in a majority of the states. As a substitute many states provide an interest for the husband similar to the dower interest granted to the wife.

The common law requirements for curtesy are as follows: (1) Lawful marriage; (2) Wife owned an estate or interest in real property which could pass by inheritance; and (3) Birth of a child capable of inheriting. The requirements are historical and have been modified in most states, where any form of the curtesy interest exists.

Where the right of curtesy or dower has been abolished or is unknown, the survivor usually takes as an heir of the deceased spouse under the laws of inheritance.

The following chart will illustrate the right of the surviving husband and wife in the real property of the deceased spouse. In the majority of cases, the interest which the surviving spouse takes is in addition to the rights of inheritance as an heir. In order to properly ascertain the complete rights of inheritance of the surviving spouse it is necessary to read the following charts in connection with the succeeding section on spouse's right of election.

RIGHT OF DOWER, CURTESY AND STATUTORY SUBSTITUTIONS

STATE	Husband	Wife
Alabama	Life estate in wife's real property and one-half of all personal property, absolutely	Life estate in 1/3 of husband's real property if husband survived by lineal descendants and life estate in 1/2 if not survived by lineal descendants
Alaska	Abolished	Abolished
Arizona	Abolished	Abolished
Arkansas	Life estate in 1/3 of wife's real property and 1/3 of all personal property absolutely[1]	Life estate in 1/3 of husband's real property and 1/3 of all personal property absolutely
California	None	None
Colorado	None	Abolished
Connecticut	None	None
Delaware	Abolished	Abolished
District of Columbia	Abolished	Abolished
Florida	Abolished	Abolished
Georgia	None	Abolished
Hawaii	Life estate in 1/3 of wife's real property and 1/3 of all personal property absolutely	Life estate in 1/3 of husband's real property and 1/3 of all personal property absolutely

31

STATE	Husband	Wife
Idaho	Abolished	None
Illinois	Abolished	Abolished
Indiana	Abolished	Abolished
Iowa	Abolished	Abolished
Kansas	One-half absolutely, of all wife's real property	One-half absolutely, of all husband's real property
Kentucky	Life estate in 1/3 of wife's real property	Life estate in 1/3 husband's real property
Louisiana	None	None
Maine	Abolished	Abolished
Maryland	Abolished	Abolished
Massachusetts	Life estate in 1/3 wife's real property	Life estate in 1/3 husband's real property
Michigan	Abolished	Life estate in 1/3 husband's real property
Minnesota	Abolished	Abolished
Mississippi	Abolished	Abolished
Missouri	Abolished	Abolished
Montana	None	Abolished
Nebraska	Abolished	Abolished
Nevada	Abolished	Abolished
New Hampshire	Abolished	Abolished
New Jersey	Life estate in 1/2 real property	Life estate in 1/2 husband's real property
New Mexico	None	None

STATE	Husband	Wife
New York	Abolished	Abolished[2]
North Carolina	Abolished	Abolished
North Dakota	None	Abolished
Ohio	Life estate in 1/3 of wife's real property	Life estate in 1/3 of husband's real property
Oklahoma	Abolished	Abolished
Oregon	Abolished	Abolished
Pennsylvania	None	None
Rhode Island	Life estate in all wife's real property	Life estate in 1/3 of husband's real property
South Carolina	Abolished	Life estate in 1/3 of husband's real property
South Dakota	Abolished	Abolished
Tennessee	Life estate in all wife's real property	Life estate in 1/3 of husband's real property
Texas	None	None
Utah	Abolished	One-third, in value, of all husband's real property[3]
Vermont	One-third in value of wife's real property[4]	One-third in value of husband's real property[4]
Virginia	1/3 of wife's real property	1/3 of husband's real property
Washington	Abolished	Abolished

STATE	Husband	Wife
West Virginia	Life estate in 1/3 of wife's real property	Life estate in 1/3 of husband's real property
Wisconsin	Life estate in 1/3 of property owned by wife at death	Life estate in 1/3 of husband's real property
Wyoming	Abolished	Abolished

---

[1] Husband's interest may be defeated by will or conveyance by his wife.
[2] Wife takes a life estate in 1/3 husband's real property if marriage and ownership of property took place prior to September 1, 1930.
[3] See Uniform Probate Code, effective July 1, 1977 (75-1-1-1 et seq).
[4] Surviving spouse entitled to ½ in value of the real property if decedent was survived by issue or heir by adoption.

where dower or curtesy exists all rights of inheritance are subject to such rights of the surviving spouse.

At common law, real estate did not descend to the surviving spouse, but only to the heirs of the deceased. The right to any real estate of the deceased existed only by virtue of the right of dower or curtesy. To a limited extent, the surviving spouse shared in the personal property.

The surviving spouse in many states has a right of inheritance in the estate of the deceased in addition to any dower or curtesy right. The right of inheritance is statutory as the spouse is not strictly speaking, the heir or next of kin of the decedent. The amount or share which the spouse takes is usually dependent on the number of children or their descendants who survive and also whether or not the deceased was survived by parents, brothers or sisters or their descendants.

Some jurisdictions provide for an inheritance as an alternative to dower or curtesy, the spouse being required to elect. Where dower and curtesy no longer exist, the spouse usually takes under the laws of inheritance, which provide for the descent and distribution of all real and personal property.

The question arises as to the distinction between the case where the spouse receives a dower or curtesy share plus an interest in the estate under the laws of inheritance, and the case where only an interest under the laws of inheritance is taken and no right of dower or curtesy exists. The right of dower or curtesy is an interest in real property, which may be defeated or barred. The right cannot usually be defeated by the mere conveyance of the property by one spouse alone. It is an interest which is inchoate during the lifetime of both, and accrues absolutely on the death of the spouse. The right to take under the laws of inheritance, on the other hand, accrues on the death of the spouse, and only affects such property. which was owned by the decedent at his death, subject to certain rights and liabilities as outlined by the statutes.

With reference to the rights of the surviving spouse in the several states, it must be noted that the share taken under the laws of inheritance is usually in addition to any right of dower or curtesy if such right exists, unless the statute provides that an election between the share must be made. Where the rights of the surviving spouse are dependent on the existence of issue or lineal descendants, the statutes usually construe the words to mean any children, grand-children, great-grand children, etc, down the line of direct lineal descendants.

RIGHT OF ELECTION: a. **Dower or Curtesy and Intestate Share:** Under many statutes which allow dower or curtesy, the spouse is granted the right to elect between the share taken by dower or curtesy and a certain distributive or intestate share. The statutes provide which share shall be taken, if an election is not made; the time within which the election must be made varies from state to state. The election must generally be exercised by the surviving spouse, during his or her lifetime.

b. Election Between Will and Distributive Share: Neither spouse may disinherit the other, in most states. Where one spouse dies leaving a Will which fails to provide for the survivor in any way, or provides a lesser amount than would have been taken had the testator died without a Will, the survivor may take the property under the Will or exercise a right of election. The right of election permits the survivor to elect to take the distributive share provided by law, as against that which would have been taken under the Will.

In some states the surviving husband has no right of election, while the widow may elect; many states allow either spouse the right to elect, although the shares taken may be different. In states where common law dower or curtesy or their statutory substitute has been retained, a testator cannot defeat by Will the share which the survivor would take. In some states the surviving spouse takes a share in the personal property in addition to dower or curtesy; while other states provide for intestate share to the survivor.

The prohibition against disinheritance by a testator is

not absolute, even in states where the spouse has a right of election. The misconduct of the surviving spouse may effectively bar the right of election. In Connecticut, abandonment continuing to the time of the testator's death, without sufficient cause, results in a forfeiture of the statutory share of inheritance. Adultery, desertion or failure to support may also result in a forfeiture.

Statutes usually provide a fixed period of time during which the election must be made. The right to elect is a personal right, however, and must be exercised by the surviving spouse during his or her lifetime.

In community property states the survivor takes at least one-half of all community property even though the testator attempts to will the survivor's share to another. In North and South Dakota, the spouse apparently has no right of election.

In the following chart illustrating the Spouse's Right of Election, the shares which may be taken as against the Will are outlined. Where an intestate share is allowed, the spouse inherits the same share that would have passed if there was no Will. Limitations on the share taken by election are included in states where they exist.

Dower or Curtesy as used here denotes the share a husband or wife would take, as provided in the table "Dower, Curtesy and Statutory Substitutions" and only indicates that the survivor takes the present statutory equivalent of Dower or Curtesy.

Spouse's Right of Election

State	Election by Husband	Wife	Limitation or Share Under the Right of Election. ●Period for Filing Election
ALABAMA T. 16 §§ 18, 19	No	Yes	Intestate share; if no children or descendants limited to $50,000. ●Within 6 months after probate.

State	Election by Husband	Wife	Limitation or Share Under the Right of Election. ●Period for Filing Election
ARKANSAS	Yes, if Will executed prior to marriage	Yes	Intestate share. ●Within 1 month after expiration for filing
COLORADO Ch. 176 §37	Yes(1)	Yes(1)	One-half of entire estate. ●Within 6 months after probate.
CONNECTICUT §7309	Yes	Yes	One-third of estate for life. ●Within 2 months after expiration for filing claims.
DELAWARE §§3541, 3767, 3771, 3774	Yes	Yes	Life estate in all real property. Life estate in one-third of real property. ●No fixed time.
DISTRICT OF COLUMBIA §18-211	Yes	Yes	Intestate share. ●Within 6 months after administration granted.
FLORIDA §§731.34, 731.35	No	Yes.	Dower and one-third of all personal property. ●Within 9 months after first publication of notice to creditors.
GEORGIA §31-103	No	Yes	Dower. ●No fixed period.
ILLINOIS §§3-168, 3-169	Yes	Yes	If all children survive one-third of entire estate; if none survive one-half of entire estate. ●Within 10 months after probate.
INDIANA §§6-2332 to 2336	Yes	Yes	Intestate share. ●Within 6 months after probate.

38

State	Election by Husband	Wife	Limitation or Share Under the Right of Election. ●Period for Filing Election
IOWA §636.22	Yes	Yes	Intestate share. ●Within 60 days after probate or 6 months after notice of admission to probate.
KANSAS §59-2233	Yes	Yes	Intestate share. ●Within 6 months after purobate(2).
KENTUCKY §392.080	Yes	Yes	Intestate share. ●Within 1 year after probate.
MAINE Ch. 156 §14	Yes	Yes	Intestate share, limited to ½ of the estate. ●Within 6 months after probate.
MARYLAND §§324, 327, 328 Art. 93	Yes	Yes	Dower or intestate share in real property and up to ½ of personal property. ●Within 30 days after expiration of notice to creditors.
MASSACHUSETTS Ch. 191 §15	Yes	Yes	Intestate share limited to $10,000 plus income of excess for life. ●Within 6 months after probate.
MICHIGAN §702.69	No	Yes	Intestate share; ½ of realty absolutely and ½ subject to legacies; personal property up to $5,000 and half of remainder. ●Within 60 days after entry of order closing estate to claims.
MINNESOTA §525.212	Yes	Yes	Intestate share limited to ½ of entire estate. ●Within 6 months after probate.

State	Election by Hus-band	Wife	Limitation or Share Under the Right of Election. •Period for Filing Election
MISSISSIPPI §668	Yes	Yes	Intestate share limited to ½ of entire estate(3). •Within 6 months after probate.
MISSOURI §§469.020, 469.100, 469.150	Yes	Yes	Intestate share. •Within 12 months after probate.
MONTANA §§22-107, 22-108, 22-109	No	Yes	Dower and intestate share of personal property(4). •Within 1 year after probate.
NEBRASKA §§3-107, 3-108	Yes	Yes	Intestate share. •Within 1 year after issuance of letters testamentary.
NEW HAMPSHIRE Ch. 359 §§10 to 14 inc.	Yes	Yes	Dower or curtesy plus one-third personal property if issue survive; if no issue $7,500 plus ½ remainder(5). •Within 1 year after death of testator.
NEW JERSEY T A3 c. 37 §§1, 2	Yes	Yes	Dower; Curtesy. •Within 6 months after probate.
NEW YORK D.E.L. §18	Yes	Yes	Intestate share limited to ½ of net estate. •Within 6 months after issuance of letters testamentary or letters of administration with Will annexed.
NORTH CAROLINA §§30-1, 30-2	No(6)	Yes	Intestate share. •Within 6 months after probate.
OHIO §10504-55	Yes	Yes	Intestate share limited to ½ of estate. •Within 1 month after service of citation to elect, if no citation is-

State	Election by Husband	Wife	Limitation or Share Under the Right of Election. ●Period for Filing Election
			sued within 9 months after appointment of executor or administrator.
OKLAHOMA T. 84 §44	Yes	Yes	Intestate share(7). ●No fixed period.
OREGON §§17-113, 17-401; L. 1949 ch. 457 L. 1951 ch. 386	Yes	Yes	Dower or curtesy in real property plus an undivided one-fourth interest in personal property. ●Real property: within year after death. Personal property: within 90 days after probate.
PENNSYLVANIA T. 20 §§180.8, 180.11	Yes	Yes	Intestate share. ●Within 1 year after probate.
RHODE ISLAND Ch. 566 §§12, 21	Yes	Yes	Dower or curtesy. ●Within 6 months after probate.
SOUTH CAROLINA 154 S.C. 64		Yes	Dower. ●Prior to distribution of estate.
TENNESSEE §§8358, 8359, 8360	Yes	Yes	Dower or curtesy plus one-third of personal property if no child or not more than two survive; a child's part of personal property if more than two children survive. ●Within 9 months after probate of will.
UTAH §§74-4-3, 74-4-4	No	Yes	Dower(8). ●Within months after probate.
VERMONT §§3031, 3041		Yes	Dower or curtesy. ●Within 8 months after probate.

41

State	Election by Husband	Wife	Limitation or Share Under the Right of Election •Period for Filing Election
VIRGINIA §§64-13, 64-16, 64-23, 64-32	Yes	Yes	Dower or curtesy and intestate share in personal property up to one-half. •Within 1 year after death or probate.
WEST VIRGINIA §§4091, 4103	Yes	Yes	Dower or curtesy and one-third of the personal property. •Within 8 months after death.
WISCONSIN §§233.13, 233.14	No	Yes	Dower and up to one-third of the personal property. •Within 1 year after probate.
WYOMING §6-301	Yes	Yes	Intestate share of entire estate, limited to ¼ of children survive; ½ if no children survive. •Within 6 months after probate.

Footnotes

(1) Survivor may elect if testator attempts to Will away more than one half of the estate.

(2) If Will admitted to probate after June 30, 1951 survivor elects to take under intestate laws; if Will admitted prior to that date survivor must elect to take under Will, failure to so elect results in inheritance of intestate share.

(3) If the surviving spouse has separate property amounting to more than a one-fifth share of the estate, the survivor can only elect to take the difference between the seperate property and the share entitled under the election (§670).

(4) Widow may take one-half of realty absolutely, in lieu of dower, if no issue survive decedent.

(5) Survivor may waive dower or curtesy and take in lieu thereof, one-third of realty if issue survive; $7,500 plus one-half of excess if no issue survive.

(6) Surviving husband takes curtesy (§52-16).

(7) Survivor may will away half the property not acquired by joint industry during the marriage.

(8) Widow presumed to take distributive share unless she elects to take under the Will.

EFFECT OF DIVORCE, SEPARATION AND AN-
NULMENT: a. **Divorce:** A decree of absolute divorce terminates the marital relationship and deprives each spouse
of any right to inherit any property from the other under
the laws of intestacy. The divorce decree must be final.
An interlocutory decree which requires that a period of
time must elapse before the decree is final does not affect
the inheritance rights of either spouse.

b. **Separation:** Where a husband and wife are living
apart at the time that one of them dies, the survivor is not
precluded from inheriting from the deceased spouse. This
rule does not necessarily apply where one spouse abandons
the other without just cause. The separation of husband
and wife, whether or not judicially decreed, does not dissolve the marriage. A husband and wife may enter into a
separation agreement, in most jurisdictions, and release to
each other any rights of inheritance which may accrue.
Where such a valid contract is entered into, the surviving
spouse will be barred from inheriting from the estate of
the decedent. A separation agreement which is subsequently abrogated by a reconciliation of husband and wife,
does not prevent either spouse from sharing in the estate
of the other.

c. **Annulment:** An annulment is a judicial declaration
that a voidable marriage no longer exists; therefore neither
party has any rights of inheritance in the estate of the
other. If the marriage is voidable but no annulment was
obtained, the parties will inherit from each other as husband and wife. If a marriage is void, the relationship of
husband and wife never existed, and no right to share in
each other's estate as husband and wife would exist.

INHERITANCE (by state)

ALABAMA **Real Property:** If there are no children, or
descendants, and no parent, brother, sister or descendants
of deceased brothers or sisters, all real property is inherited
by the surviving husband or wife (T. 16 §1). In any case,

the surviving husband receives a life estate in all real property owned by the wife at her death (T. 16 §12). The surviving wife shares in the real property by her dower right.

Personal Property: (a) Wife's Share—If no children survive the decedent the wife takes all; if survived by one child she takes one-half; if the decedent is survived by two, three or four children the wife receives a child's share; if five or more children survive, the wife receives one-fifth (T. 16 §10). If the separate property owned by the wife, at her husband's death is equal to or exceeds her share of the estate, she is barred from receiving any part of the estate (T. 16 §42); if her separate property is less than her share, her inheritance is reduced by the amount of her separate property (T. 16 §43). (b) Husband's Share—One-half of all the personal property (T. 16 §12).

ARIZONA Community Property: Upon the death of the husband or wife one-half of the community property shall go to the survivor. If the decedent is not survived by descendants, the surviving spouse inherits all the community property (§39-109).

Separate Property: If the decedent is survived by children or descendants, the spouse inherits one-third of the personal estate and takes a life estate in one-third of the real property. If the decedent is survived by a parent but no descendants the spouse inherits the entire personal estate and one-half of the real property. The surviving spouse inherits the entire estate where the decedent is not survived by descendants nor parents (§39-102).

ARKANSAS In addition to dower and curtesy the surviving spouse inherits one-third of the personal estate (§61-202). If no descendants survive the decedent, the spouse inherits one-half of the entire estate; part of which is subject to the right of creditors (§61-206, 228). If there be no children or their descendants, parents nor their descendants or any paternal or maternal kindred, the surviving spouse inherits the entire estate (§61-107).

44

CALIFORNIA **Community Property:** Upon the death of husband or wife, one-half of the community property goes to the survivor. If the other half is not disposed of by Will, it goes to the survivor (Prob. C. §201).

Separate Property: The surviving spouse inherits as follows—One-half of the entire estate if the decedent leaves one child or the issue of a deceased child; one-third, if the decedent leaves more than one child, or one child and the issue of one or more deceased children (Prob. C §221). The spouse takes one-half, if the decedent leaves no issue but is survived by either parent, brothers or sisters or their descendants (Prob. C. §223). The spouse inherits the entire estate if neither issue, parent, brother, sister, nor descendant of deceased brother or sister, survive the decedent (Prob. C. §224).

COLORADO The surviving spouse inherits one-half of the estate if the decedent is survived by children or their descendants; if no children or descendants of any child survive, the surviving spouse inherits the entire estate (ch. 176 §1).

CONNECTICUT The surviving spouse inherits one-third of the estate if the decedent is survived by children or descendants of deceased children. If the decedent is survived by a parent but no children or their representatives, the spouse inherits the whole estate up to $5,000, and one-half of the balance. The spouse inherits the entire estate if the decedent is survived by no children or representatives of children and no parent (§7309 as amend. L. 1951 P.A. 372).

DELAWARE In addition to dower and curtesy, the surviving spouse inherits as follows: **Real Property:** If the decedent leaves no heirs or next of kin surviving, the surviving spouse inherits all real property (§3731). **Personal Property:** The spouse inherits one-third of the personal property, if the decedent is survived by children or their descendants; the surviving spouse inherits all personal property if no children nor descendants survive (§3847).

45

DISTRICT OF COLUMBIA Real Property: The surviving spouse takes dower or curtesy in real property. The surviving spouse inherits all real property if the decedent is survived by no children, or descendants, parent, brother, sister or descendants of deceased brothers or sisters (§18-101). **Personal Property:** The surviving spouse inherits one-third of all personal property if decedent is survived by a child or descendants (§18-703). If the decedent is survived by no child or descendants but by either parent, and brother, sister or children of deceased brothers or sisters, the spouse inherits one-half. If the decedent is survived by none of the above mentioned, the spouse inherits all personal property.

FLORIDA The surviving spouse inherits a child's share of the entire estate if the decedent is survived by lineal descendants. If no lineal descendants survive the decedent, the surviving spouse inherits the entire estate (§731.23). The widow must elect to take her dower share as against her statutory share as a surviving spouse.

GEORGIA The surviving spouse inherits a child's share of the entire estate if the decedent is survived by children or their descendants; however, if there are more than five shares, the widow is entitled to one-fifth. The surviving spouse inherits the entire estate if the decedent leaves no children or descendants (§113-901). The widow must elect between dower and her distributive share in the real property of the estate. The right of election does not affect her inheritance of personal property.

IDAHO The surviving spouse inherits the following share of the entire estate; one-third, if the decedent is survived by two children or one child and issue of a deceased child or issue of two or more deceased children; one-half, if the decedent is survived by one child or issue of one deceased child or father or mother. The surviving spouse inherits the entire estate if the decedent is survived by neither issue or parent (§14-103).

ILLINOIS The surviving spouse takes the following

share of real and personal property; one-third if the decedent is survived by descendants; all personal property and one-half of the real property if the decedent is survived by no issue but parents, brother or sister or their descendants. The surviving spouse inherits the entire estate where decedent was not survived by descendants, parent, brother, sister or descendants of brothers and sisters (ch. 3 §162). The surviving spouse is required to elect between a dower interest in real property, and the share as outlined above. The spouse takes a distributive share of real property in which dower was not perfected.

INDIANA **Real Property:** The widow inherits one-half of the real property if decedent is survived by one child or descendant (§6-2314). If the decedent is survived by more than one child or descendant, the widow merits one-third of the real property, provided, that if the value of the real estate exceeds $10,000, the wido wtakes one-fourth as against creditors and if the value exceeds $20,000, she takes one-fifth as against creditors (§6-2313). The surviving husband inherits one-third of the real property if issue survive the decedent (§6-2321).

Personal Property: The widow inherits a child's share of the personal property, but not less than one-third, if the decedent is survived by children or descendants (§6-2320). The husband inherits one-third of the personal property if decedent is survived by issue (§-2322).

The surviving spouse inherits three-fourths of the entire estate if the decedent is survived by mother or father, but no child (§-2323). The entire estate passes to the surviving spouse if the decedent died leaving no child or parent (§6-2324).

IOWA In addition to dower or curtesy, the surviving spouse inherits the whole estate up to $15,000 and one-half of the excess if no issue survive the decedent (§636.32). The surviving spouse inherits the entire estate if the decedent leaves no issue, no parent nor heirs of any parent (§§636.40, 636.41).

KANSAS: In addition to dower or curtesy, the surviving spouse inherits one-half of the entire estate if the decedent is survived by a child or children or issue of a previously deceased child or children. The surviving spouse inherits the entire estate if the decedent was survived by no child or children or issue of a previously deceased child (§59-504).

KENTUCKY In addition to dower or curtesy, the surviving spouse inherits one-half of all personal property (§392.020). The survivor inherits the entire estate if the decedent is survived by neither paternal or maternal kindred (§391.010).

LOUISIANA Community Property: Upon the death of either spouse, one-half of the community property belongs to the survivor. The survivor takes one-half of community property undisposed of by Will if the decedent is survived by either mother or father but no descendants (C.C. 915). The survivor takes all undisposed community property if the decedent is survived by neither father, mother nor descendants (C.C. 915). The widow takes a usufruct (i. e., the use of real property) in a child's share if left with a child. The interest ceases when a second marriage is contracted (C.C. 916). Separate Property: The surviving spouse inherits all separate property if decedent left no lawful descendants, ascendants or collateral relatives; provided that the widower is so entitled only when the wife, in addition to above, leaves no natural child, or children duly acknowledged by her (C.C. 924).

MAINE: The surviving spouse inherits one-third of the estate if the decedent is survived by issue. If the decedent leaves no issue the survivor inherits one-half of the estate, provided, however, that if they were living together at death, the survivor takes $5,000 and one-half of the remainder of the estate. If no kindred survive, the survivor takes the entire estate (c. 156 §1). Dower and curtesy have been abolished; however, the one-third interest of the survivor in real property attaches to all real property owned

48

during the marriage, which interest was not conveyed, released or barred.

MARYLAND Surviving spouse inherits an intestate share of real property unless an election to take dower or curtesy is made within six months after death (art. 46, §§1, 3). The surviving spouse inherits the following share of real property (if no election is made) and personal property: One-third, if decedent is survived by a child, children or descendants of a predeceased child or children (art. 93, §130). One-half if decedent is survived by a parent or parents, but no issue (art. 93, §131). The survivor inherits the whole estate up to $2,000 and one-half of the excess, if decedent is survived by a brother, sister or child of a deceased brother or sister, and no issue or parent (art. 93, §131). If the decedent is survived by none of the above mentioned, the survivor inherits the entire estate (art. 93, §129).

MASSACHUSETTS The surviving spouse inherits an intestate share of the estate unless an election to take dower or curtesy is made within six months after the date of the administrator's or executor's bond (ch. 189, §1). The survivor's intestate share is as follows: One-third of the estate if the decedent is survived by issue; $10,000 and one-half of the excess if kindred but no issue survive the decedent. If no kindred survive, the survivor inherits the entire estate (ch. 190, §1).

MICHIGAN The widow inherits an intestate share of the decedent's real property unless she elects to take dower within 60 days after the entry of order closing estate to claims (§702-70). The surviving spouse inherits the following intestate share of real and personal property; One-third of the estate if the children or issue of a deceased child or children survive the decedent; one-half of the estate if one child or issue of one deceased child survive the decedent. The surviving husband inherits one-half of the estate if no issue but a parent, brother, sister or children of a deceased brother or sister survive the decedent. If the decedent is survived by a parent, brothers, sisters or children of deceased brothers or sisters the widow inherits $3,000 and one-half of the balance of the estate. If no issue, parent, brother, sister or children of a deceased brother or sister survive the decedent, the surviving spouse inherits the entire estate (§702.93).

MINNESOTA The surviving spouse inherits one-third of the estate if more than one child or one child and issue of a deceased child or issue of two or more deceased children survive the decedent. If the decedent is survived by one child or the issue of one deceased child, the surviving spouse inherits one-half of the estate. If no issue or descendants survive the decedent, the survivor inherits the entire estate (§525.16). The surviving spouse takes the above-mentioned proportionate interest in all real property of which the decedent, while married to such spouse, we seized or possessed, to the disposition whereof such survivor shall not have consented in writing (§525.16).

MISSISSIPPI If children or their descendants survive the decedent, the surviving spouse inherits a child's share. If no children or descendants survive the decedent, the survivor inherits the entire estate (§§470, 472).

MISSOURI The surviving spouse inherits, in addition to dower or curtesy, a child's share of the personal property, if the decedent dies leaving a child, children or other descendants (§469.070). When the husband shall die without any child or other descendants his widow shall be entitled: (1) to all the real and personal estate which came to the husband in right of the marriage and all personal property, and to all the personal property which came to his possession with the written assent of the wife not subject to his debts; (2) to one-half of the real and personal estate belonging to the husband at the time of his death, absolutely, subject to the payment of the husband's debts (§469.090). When a wife shall dies without any child or other descendants, her widower shall be entitled to one-half of the real and personal estate belonging to the wife at the time of her death absolutely, subject to the payment of the wife's debts (§469.130). The surviving spouse may elect to take a child's share in real property, in lieu of dower, if the decedent is survived by children or descendants (§§469.-020, 469.080). The surviving spouse inherits the entire estatre, if the decedent is survived by neither child or descendant, parent, brother,sister or descendants of deceased brothers or sisters (§469.010).

MONTANA The widow takes dower in addition to her rights as heir under intestacy (28 Mont. 37). The surviving spouse inherits one-third of the estate, if the decedent is survived by more than one child or one child and issue of a deceased child or issue of more than one deceased child. If the decedent is survived by one child or the lawful issue of one child, the surviving spouse inherits one-half of the estate. If the decedent leaves no issue, entire estate goes to the surviving husband or wife (§91-403).

NEBRASKA The surviving spouse who is the parent of all children of the decedent inherits as follows: One-third of the estate if two or more children or one child and issue of one deceased child or issue of two or more deceased children survive the decedent. One-half if one child or issue of one deceased child survive the decedent. The survivor who is not the parent of all children of the deceased inherits one-fourth of the estate if one or more children or issue of one or more deceased children survive the decedent. The survivor inherits one-half of the estate if the decedent is survived by blood relatives and the entire estate, if none survive (§30-101).

The surviving spouse takes the above proportionate share in all real estate which the deceased owned at anytime during the marriage and not conveyed by the husband and wife, subject to the debts of the decedent (§30-101).

NEVADA Community Property: The surviving husband is entitled to all of the community property except that if the husband abandons his wife, he is only entitled to one-half (§3395.01). The surviving wife is entitled to one-half of the community property; if the decedent is not survived by children, the widow takes all, subject to any testamentary disposition over one-half (§3395.02).

Separate Property: The surviving spouse inherits the following share, subject to the decedent's debts: One-third, if more than one child or one child and descendants of one deceased child or descendants of two or more deceased children survive the decedent. The survivor inherits one-half, if one child, descendants of deceased child, parent, brother, sister or issue of a deceased brother or sister survive the decedent. If none of the last mentioned relatives survive, the spouse inherits all separate property (§982.-297).

NEW HAMPSHIRE **Real Property:** The widow takes her dower share unless it is waived, in which case the following intestate share is inherited: One-third if the decedent is survived by issue. If no issue survive the decedent, the widow inherits $10,000 and one-half of the excess (ch. 359, §11, Amend. L. 1951 ch. 29). The surviving husband takes his curtesy share unless it is waived, in which case he inherits one-third if issue, by him, survive. The surviving husband takes a life estate in one-third of all real property if issue by the wife and not by the widower survive and he takes no estate by the curtesy. The widower inherits $10,000 and one-half of the excess, if no issue survive (ch. 359, §11, Amend. L. 1951 ch. 29).

Personal Property: In addition to an inheritance in real property, the surviving spouse inherits one-third of all personal property if issue survive the decedent. The survivor inherits $10,000 and one-half of the excess if no issue survive (ch. 359, §§10, 12; Amend. L. 1951 ch. 29).

NEW JERSEY In addition to dower or curtesy, the surviving spouse inherits the following share: One-third of all personal property if the decedent is survived by children or descendants (T. 3A §4-2). If the decedent is not survived

52

by children or descendants, the surviving spouse inherits the entire estate (T. 3A §4-3).

NEW MEXICO **Community Property:** Upon the death of the wife, the entire community property belongs to the husband (§31-108). Upon the death of the husband one-half of the community property goes to the surviving wife and the other half is subject to the testamentary disposition of the husband; in the absence of such testamentary disposition the wife takes one-fourth if issue survive the decedent; and all, if no issue survive (§31-108). **Separate Property:** The surviving spouse inherits one-fourth of all separate property if issue survive the decedent (§31-110). If no issue survive, the survivor inherits the whole estate (§31-113).

NEW YORK The surviving spouse inherits one-third of the entire estate if children or descendants survive the decedent. If the decedent is survived by a parent but no issue, the survivor takes $5,000 and one-half of the excess. If the decedent is survived by neither issue nor parent but by brothers, sisters or their descendants, the survivor takes $10,000 and one-half of the excess. The surviving spouse inherits the entire estate if the decedent is survived by neither children, descendants, parents, brothers, sister, niece or nephew (D.E.L. §83).

NORTH CAROLINA The surviving spouse takes dower or curtesy in real property. Personal property is distributed as follows: **Widow**—If the decedent is survived by one child or descendants of a deceased child the widow inherits one-half of the personal property. If more than one child or one child and the issue of one or more deceased children or issue of two or more deceased children survive the decedent, the widow inherits a child's share. If no issue but next of kin survive, the widow inherits $10,000 and one-half of the remainder. The widow inherits all personal property if no issue nor next of kin survive. **Husband**—One-half of the personal property is inherited by the husband where the decedent is survived by one child or descendants of a deceased child. If more than one child or one child and the issue of one or more deceased children or issue of two or more deceased children survive the decedent, the husband inherits a child's share. Where no children or descendants survive, the husband inherits all the personal property (§29-149).

When a husband or wife shall die leaving no heirs surviving, the surviving spouse inherits all real and personal property of the estate (§29-1, Rule 8).

NORTH DAKOTA The surviving spouse inherits one-third of the entire estate if the decedent is survived by more than one child or one child and the lawful issue of one or more deceased children. If the decedent is survived by one child or the lawful issue of one deceased child, the surviving spouse takes one-half of the estate. If the decedent is not survived by issue the surviving spouse inherits $15,000 and one-half of the excess if either parent survive the decedent. If the decedent leaves no issue or parent and the estate does not exceed $50,000 the whole thereof goes to the surviving spouse. If the decedent is not survived by issue or parent but leaves brothers, sisters or children of deceased brothers or sisters the spouse takes $25,000 and one-half of the excess. If the decedent is survived by neither issue, parent, brothers, sisters nor children of deceased brothers or sisters, the whole estate goes to the surviving spouse (§56-0104).

OHIO The surviving husband or wife takes dower only in those lands which were conveyed or incumbered during the lifetime of both, without the consent of the other spouse. There is no vested dower in lands owned by the decedent at his death. In lieu of such dower interest as terminates and is barred, pursuant to the statutes, the surviving spouse is entitled to the intestate share provided by the laws of inheritance (§10502-1).

The surviving spouse inherits the following intestate share: If there be a spouse and one child or its descendants, surviving, one-half to the surviving spouse. If there be a spouse and more than one child or their descendants,

54

one-third to the surviving spouse. If there be no children or descendants but parents surviving, the spouse inherits three-fourths. If no children or their descendants nor parent survive, the surviving spouse inherits the entire estate (§10503-4).

OKLAHOMA The surviving spouse inherits one-half of the entire estate if the decedent is survived by one child or the issue of one deceased child. If the decedent is survived by more than one child or one child and the issue of one deceased child or issue of two or more deceased children, the spouse takes one-third. However, if the decedent was married more than once, the spouse at death takes only a child's share with living children and issue of deceased children in that property which was not acquired during the marriage. If no issue but a parent, brother or sister survive the decedent, the surviving spouse inherits one-half. However, the survivor inherits all property which was acquired during the marriage by the joint industry of husband and wife, if the decedent is not survived by issue. The surviving spouse takes the entire estate if neither issue, parent, brother or sister survive the decedent (84, §213).

OREGON The surviving spouse takes dower or curtesy in real property; if the decedent is not survived by lineal descendants, the survivor inherits all real property (§16-601). The spouse inherits one-half of all personal property if issue survive; all personal property if no issue survive the decedent (§16-102).

PENNSYLVANIA The surviving spouse inherits one-third of the entire estate if the decedent is survived by more than one child or one child and the issue of a deceased child or issue of more than one deceased child. If the decedent is survived by one child or the issue of one deceased child the survivor inherits one-half of the excess if no issue survive the decedent. The surviving spouse inherits all of the estate if the decedent is survived by no issue, parent, brother, sister, child of a brother or sister,

55

grandparent, uncle or aunt (T. 20, §1.2). The wife takes her proportionate interstate share in all real property which her husband owned at his death or which was conveyed by him without her joining in the conveyance (T. 20, §1.5(A).

RHODE ISLAND In addition to dower or curtesy in real property, the surviving spouse takes one-half of the personal property if the decedent is survived by issue (ch. 567, §9). If no issue survive the decedent, the survivor takes $3,000 and one-half of personal property and a life estate in all real property (ch. 567, §§4, 9). If the decedent is survived by neither maternal nor paternal kindred, the surviving spouse takes the entire estate (ch. 567, §4).

SOUTH CAROLINA The widow takes dower unless she accepts her distributive share of the estate which, if accepted, is in lieu of and is in bar of dower. If the widow forfeits her dower she shall also forfeit her intestate share of her husband's real property (§§19-57, 151).

Subject to the exceptions above, the surviving spouse inherits the following share of all real and personal property: One-half if the decedent is survived by one child or descendants of a deceased child; one-third if the decedent is survived by more than one child or their descendants. The surviving spouse inherits one-half of the estate if decedent is survived by no children or issue but was survived by a parent or other ancestor, brother, sister, nephew or niece, of either whole or half blood. The survivor inherits the entire estate if none of the above mentioned survive the decedent (§19-52).

SOUTH DAKOTA If the decedent leaves a surviving spouse and more than one child or one child and the issue of a deceased child or the issue of two or more deceased children, the survivor inherits one-third of the estate. If one child or the issue of a deceased child survive the decedent, the surviving spouse inherits one-half of the estate. The spouse inherits $20,000 and one-half of the excess, if decedent is survived by no issue but a parent, brother or sister or descendants of deceased brothers and sisters. If the decedent leaves a surviving husband or wife and no issue, and no parent nor brother, nor sister, the whole estate shall go to the surviving husband or wife (§56.0104).

TENNESSEE In addition to dower or curtesy, the surviving spouse takes the following share: **Personal Property:** If decedent is survived by children or descendants the surviving spouse inherits a child's share of all personal property. If no children or descendants survive, the surviving spouse inherits all of the personal estate (§8389). **Real Property:** If the decedent leaves no heirs at law capable of inheriting real estate, it passes to the surviving spouse (§8382).

TEXAS **Community Property:** On the death of either husband or wife, all community property passes to the survivor, if the decedent is survived by neither children or descendants. If the decedent is survived by any children or descendants, the surviving spouse takes one half of the community property (§2578). **Separate Property:** If the deceased leaves a child, children, or descendants, the surviving husband or wife takes one-third of the personal estate and a life estate in one-third of real property. If no children or descendants survive the decedent, the spouse inherits all of the personal property and one-half of all real property absolutely. If the deceased has neither issue, parent, brothers, sisters nor their descendants surviving, the entire estate passes to the surviving spouse (§2571).

UTAH The widow takes a dower interest in real property. The share which is inherited as surviving spouse includes her dower interest, and is not in addition to dower (§74-4-3).

The surviving spouse inherits one-third of all real and personal property if the decedent is survived by one child or the issue of one deceased child. If more than one child or one child and the issue of a deceased child or issue of more than one deceased child survive the decedent, the spouse inherits one-third of the estate. The surviving spouse takes the whole estate up to $25,000, exclusive of debts and expenses, and one-half of the excess, if no issue but a parent, brother, sister or children or grand-children of a deceased brother or sister survive the decedent. If none of the above mentioned survive the decedent, the spouse inherits the entire estate.

VERMONT The surviving spouse takes dower or curtesy. Where the decedent is not survived by issue, the survivor takes an intestate share unless an election to take dower or curtesy is made within eight months after letters of administration are issued (§3031). The survivor inherits the whole estate up to $4,000 and one-half of the excess, if no issue survive. If the decedent has no kindred surviving, the spouse is entitled to the entire estate (§3042).

VIRGINIA The surviving spouse takes a dower or curtesy interest in real property. If the decedent is survived by a child or descendants the surviving spouse inherits one-third of the personal property. If no children or descendants survive, the surviving husband or wife is entitled to all personal property of the estate (§64-11).

WASHINGTON Community Property: Upon the death of either husband or wife, one half of the community property shall go to the survivor. If no testamentary disposition is made of the remainder, and no issue or descendants survive the decedent, the remainder of the community property passes to the surviving spouse. Separate Property— Real Property: The surviving spouse inherits one-third of all separate real property if more than one child or one child and the lawful issue of one or more deceased children or lawful issue of more than one deceased child survive the decedent. If the decedent is survived by one child or the lawful issue of a deceased child or parent, brother, sister, nephew or niece, the surviving spouse takes one-half of all separate real property. If none of the above mentioned survive, the survivor takes all real property

58

(§11.04.020). **Personal Property:** If the decedent left issue the surviving spouse inherits one-half of the personal property; if no issue survive, the spouse takes all personal property (§11.04.030).

WEST VIRGINIA **Real Property:** In addition to dower or curtesy, the surviving spouse takes the following share of real property: If the decedent leaves no issue but is survived by a parent and brothers, sisters or descendants of deceased brothers and sisters, the surviving spouse inherits one-fourth of the real property. If the decedent leaves no children or parent but is survived by a brother, sister or descendant of a deceased brother or sister, the surviving spouse takes one-half of the real property. If the decedent is survived by none of the above mentioned, the survivor inherits all real property (§4080). **Personal Property:** If the decedent is survived by issue, the survivor inherits one-third; if no issue survive, the surviving spouse inherits all personal property (§4089).

WISCONSIN The surviving spouse takes an intestate share in personal property in addition to dower or curtesy in real property. If one child or descendant of a deceased child survives the decedent, the surviving spouse inherits one-half of all personal property. In all other cases the spouse is entitled to one-third of the personal property. If no children or other lineal descendants survive the decedent, the surviving spouse inherits all real and personal property of the estate (§237.01).

WYOMING The surviving spouse inherits one-half of the entire estate, if the decedent is survived by children or descendants. If no descendants but a parent, brother or sister survive the decedent, the spouse takes the whole estate up to $20,000 and three-fourths of the excess. If there be none of the aforementioned relatives of the intestate, the surviving spouse inherits the entire estate (§6-2501).

Chapter V

GETTING DIVORCED

All states prescribe precisely the terms under which the marriage contract may be terminated. All are based on the principles that the state should preserve the stability of marriage and should protect all parties insofar as it is possible to do so by legal means.

In the past, divorce was always an adversary proceeding in which one partner sued the other for the divorce, alleging some fault that corresponded to the "grounds" for divorce listed in the state law. In a few states, this form of proceeding is still required. In most, other options are available.

The grounds for divorce most often included in the state laws are: cruelty, adultery, impotency, incurable insanity, desertion, abandonment or neglect (for specified periods), habitual drunkenness, use of drugs, imprisonment, and conviction for a felony. In a traditional divorce action, the divorce is granted only if the party sued is found to be at fault in relation to the ground alleged. This is true even if the petition for divorce is not contested.

In recent years, laws have been enacted in most states which are designed to eliminate findings of fault in divorce cases. These laws have been generally labeled no-fault, but they differ from state to state. New York now permits a husband and wife to divorce if they have been voluntarily living apart, with legal papers to prove it, for at least two years. Until 1967 New York would accept no grounds for divorce other than adultery. California's 1970 legislation established only two grounds for divorce (or marital dissolution, as it is called there and in other states with similar no fault laws): incurable insanity or irreconcilable differences. The latter phrase simply means that if husband and wife do not get along together, for whatever reason, society does not deny them the right to return to their single status.

Maine and 17 other states have *added* no-fault grounds to

to the longtime grounds for divorce still set forth in the statutes.

Custody of Children

Under early common law, fathers had the legal right to the custody of children. In modern times the rights of the mother came to be more widely recognized and favored. In some states, laws specifically state that young children are best cared for by the mother. Some of these laws have been challenged. In Florida this notion has changed: "Upon considering all relevant factors, the father of the child shall be given the same considerations as the mother in determining custody." Women can no longer take for granted their custody rights as a mother.

In disputed cases when the court must decide on custody, the judge hears evidence concerning the fitness of parents. In California and other states which have adopted no-fault divorce laws, evidence of misconduct by either parent may be admitted in the custody proceedings "provided the acts are relevant to the issue of custodial competence."

In most cases, custody is granted to one parent with visiting rights to the other, Visitation rights to grandparents may also be granted in many states.

A judge may, in a divorce proceeding, also appoint independent parties to represent the interest of children who are involved. Such appointees are usually called guardians ad litem.

Alimony

Alimony is considered a continuation of the support obligation assumed by the husband at the time of the marriage. By statute, only the wife is permitted to receive alimony in eighteen states and the District of Columbia; in all others, either spouse is eligible.

The amount of alimony award usually depends on the life style to which the couple has become accustomed; the length of the marriage; age; health; children responsibilities; financial status; and potential for employment. In a number of states a spouse who wins a divorce because of the other's adultery is not obligated to pay, no matter how great the other spouse's need.

If an ex-wife wants to remarry, she will usually have to give up her alimony, since it is a continuation of a husband's obligation to support. The spouse receiving alimony payments must report them as income; the one making the payments is entitled to claim them as deductions.

Property Settlement

In the community property states, each spouse is generally entitled to half the community property at the time of the divorce, although there are some variations depending upon the grounds for divorce.

The great majority of states-both common law and community property-authorize the courts to divide the property in a divorce action according to what it decides is just. In this way many courts in common law states have come up, with results comparable to those arrived at in the community property states.

Eighteen states and the District of Columbia allow a divorcing couple to agree by contract on the marital property division and the amount and duration of the support, if any. Such a contract must be accepted by the court unless the terms are "unconscionable."

RESIDENCE REQUIREMENTS: All states have a minimum period during which person is required to be a continuous resident before a divorce may be obtained. This requirement is primarily to discourage (or encourage) residents of foreign states from shopping around for an easy jurisdiction in which to start a divorce action. Different rules may apply where the marriage was solemnized in the state; or where both parties were always residents of the state, etc.

Most of the states also have the same or similar time residence requirements in connection with annulment and separation suits.

It should also be indicated that these residence requirements may not necessarily apply where the ground for the divorce is "insanity subsequent to the marriage." Because of the unusual nature of the grounds, many states require proof of residence for the same period that the insanity must exist before it is considered as a cause for an absolute divorce.

In some states the residence requirements differ according to the ground for the action and whether the cause arose in or out of the state.

Most states today credit time served in the armed forces toward the residence period required.

The form of complaint in a divorce action is farily well standardized. It must state date and place of the marriage; names and ages of the children, if any; a statement to the effect that the plaintiff is a resident of the state in which the action is brought; the facts on which the cause of action is based; that the statutory period of limitation has not elapsed since the discovery by the plaintiff of the cause of action against the defendant; that the plaintiff has not forgiven the cause of action against the defendant and generally a statement to the effect that the plaintiff has not voluntarily cohabited with the defendant since the discovery of the cause of action; that no decree of divorce has been obtained by the defendant against the plaintiff, and that no other action for divorce between the parties is pending. In a divorce action where the wife is the plaintiff and there are no children, it is sometimes desirable to ask that she be permitted to resume her maiden name. Then, at the court hearing, the plaintiff is generally asked what her maiden name was and if she wants to resume it and if so a provision is included in the decree to that effect. The complaint must be sworn to as to the truth thereof of the facts stated by the plaintiff.

While unquestionably divorce procedure could be further simplified, even though there are fifty different divorce laws in the United States, a great deal of simplification has been accomplished in the last hundred years. The first divorces in the United States required the passage of a special law for each one by the state legislature.

The courts still insist that a divorce suit must represent

a contest, although a large percentage of divorces are amicable and have been arranged between the parties. Nevertheless, in the eyes of the law, before any decree may be entered, the court must be satisfied that it has jurisdiction of the parties and that there has been a genuinely contested divorce action. In view of present day procedure this attitude seems positively absurd and hypocritical.

When a divorce decree has been duly obtained in New York it is of course recognized by every New York court. Likewise, where a divorce is duly obtained outside of New York, where both parties are actual bona fide residents of the state or county where such divorce is obtained, New York wil recognize such a divorce as valid. But what about divorce decrees rendered outside of the state and where only one of the parties establishes a foreign residence? It is understandable that persons will seek relief where the courts are most amenable to divorce actions. Will New York recognize the validity of these "Foreign Divorce Decrees"?

FOREIGN DIVORCES: The Supreme Court of the United States has been called upon to rule on the validity of foreign divorces many times within the past few years. The question is in many respects still open to dispute. Some general principle of law, however, may be suggested as a result of these restrictions.

Assume that John and Jane were married in state X and are both residents of that state. They live happily for a while and then fall into marital difficulties. Jane leaves John, moves to state Y and starts an action for divorce. She is granted a divorce decree by the court of state Y and returns to state X. Will state X recognize this decree of its sister state? This will depend on the following circumstances:

1. Did Jane establish a legal domicile (residence) in State Y?
2. Was John personally served with the summons in State Y or did he appear in court or did he appear by an attorney or did he receive notice of the divorce action only by publication?

65

If both parties submitted to the jurisdiction of state Y and the court there found that the plaintiff had established a bona fide domicile, then the divorce decree of state Y must be recognized in state X.

If, however, the plaintiff did not make personal service of the summons on the defendant in the state but served notice on him only by publication then, even though the court of state Y found that bona fide domicile had been established, its decree is not conclusive in state X. The finding of domicile by the court in state Y is entitled to prima facie weight in the court of a sister state but does not prevent relitigation of the question there. The decree of divorce of state Y under these circumstances may be collaterally attacked in the courts of a sister state.

As a general rule, then, the law may be stated as follows:

1. Where both parties have appeared in the divorce action in state Y, the validity of its decree may not be collaterally attacked in any other state.

2. Where there has been no appearance by the defendant in the court of state Y, its divorce decree is not conclusive in state X. Persons who seek the advantages of a quick and easy divorce must remember the risk involved.

3. Where alimony, custody, counsel fees and other factors are involved, the problem is further complicated.

Estin v. Estin, 334 U.S. 541, illustrates the latter point. After five years of marriage the husband abandoned his wife in 1942. In 1943 the wife sought and was awarded (husband appearing personally in the action) a decree of separation in New York. The decree included an award of alimony. The husband then went to Nevada and instituted an action for divorce on grounds which were recognized in Nevada. The court granted the divorce decree but the wife was not personally served with the summons nor did she appear at the trial. The divorce decree made no provision for alimony. After the divorce, the husband ceased paying alimony which was still due under the separation decree of the New York court. The wife now sued the husband in New York for arrears in alimony. The husband defended on the grounds that the Nevada divorce decree ended his obligation to make further alimony payments. The New York court granted the wife a judgment of alimony arrears. This decree was subsequently affirmed in the Supreme Court of the United States.

The rationale of the case is as follows:

The Nevada divorce decree was recognized in New York so far as the marital status of the parties was concerned. New York recognized that they were now legally divorced.

But the alimony provision which had originally been awarded in the New York separation decree was a "property right" and the Nevada court could not adjudicate the wife's rights in regard to such property rights unless it had personal jurisdiction over her.

In effect then, the foreign decree was recognized by the New York court in some respects and denied validity in others.

MEXICAN DIVORCES: Before concluding the subject of divorce a word should be said regarding so-called Mexican divorces. Very often parties who cannot obtain a divorce for one reason or another in their own states try to break the bonds of matrimony by obtaining a decree in Mexico. Such divorces are frequently subject to attack.

Separation

A Separation, or as it is sometimes called, a limited divorce differs from both annulment and divorce in important respects. It is limited in the sense that the parties are still married to each other. They are merely separated from bed and board but not from the bonds of matrimony.

Suit for separation may in most states be brought by either the husband or the wife. In all cases, however, the party bringing the suit must be the party not at fault. A

67

separation suit is generally brought for permanent separate maintenance and support of the wife or the wife and children. The most common grounds are desertion or cruel and inhuman treatment. In some states the action is one which may be instituted only by the wife. Suit for a separation does not bar the complaining party from later bringing an action for absolute divorce on the same or upon additional grounds. After the parties enter into separation agreements which are filed in court at the time suit for separation is begun, such agreements are, if properly drawn, recognized by the court and in many cases, included in the decree of separation.

The separation decree sanctions the refusal of the wife to cohabit. The decree or judgment of separation may later be revoked in most of the states by either of two methods (1) By the joint application of the parties to the court upon a reconciliation, or (2) by the parties voluntarily cohabiting with each other without any formal court proceedings for revocation of the separation decree.

GROUNDS FOR ANNULMENT BY STATE

ALABAMA — None. But incestuous marriage can be avoided if either spouse is convicted of that crime.

ALASKA — Incest; bigamy. The following grounds are valid unless the marital relationship is continued after the ground no longer exists: mental incapacity at time of marriage; under age and without parental approval; fraud, force, or duress.

ARIZONA — None. But incestuous and bigamous marriage, or those where one party was without mental capacity at time of marriage, can be voided.

ARKANSAS — Mental incapacity at time of marriage; under age; fraud; force or duress; impotence at time of marriage.

CALIFORNIA — Bigamy; incurable impotence. The following grounds are valid unless the marital relationship is continued after the ground no longer exists: mental incapacity at time of marriage; under age; fraud; force or

COLORADO — Mental incapacity at time of marriage; including that caused by drugs or alcohol; fraud; duress; physical inability to perform sexual intercourse; couple got married on dare or in jest. Incestuous and bigamous marriages where void in the states where they were performed may be declared invalid.

CONNECTICUT

None. But whenever a marriage is void or voidable for any cause under the laws of Connecticut or of the state where the marriage was performed the marriage may be declared void.

DELAWARE

Bigamy; incest; incurable impotence. The following grounds are valid unless the marital relationship is continued after the ground no longer exists: under age; fraud; force or duress; insanity.

DISTRICT OF COLUMBIA

Fraud; force or duress; bigamy; impotence.

FLORIDA

None.

GEORGIA

None. But if spouses were imcompetent or fraudently induced to marry, an annulment may be granted unless there are children as a result of the marriage.

HAWAII

Mental incapacity at time of marriage; under age; fraud; force or duress; bigamy; incest; impotence; either spouse afflicted with any loathsome disease if this is unknown to the other.

IDAHO

Bigamy; incurable impotence.

ILLINOIS

Annulment may be granted, but grounds are not ennumerated in statute.

INDIANA

Mental incapacity at time of mar-

70

riage; under age; fraud; bigamy; incest.

IOWA

Mental incapacity at time of marriage; impotence at time of marriage; marriage prohibited by law.

KANSAS

Fraud; bigamy; impotence at time of marriage; wife pregnant by another at time of marriage without husband's knowledge.

KENTUCKY

Mental incapacity at time of marriage, including that caused by drugs or alcohol; fraud; force or duress; physical inability to perform sexual intercourse; marriage prohibited by law.

LOUISIANA

Duress is valid unless the marital relationship is continued after the ground no longer exists.

MAINE

Mental incapacity at time of marriage; bigamy; incest; life imprisonment.

MARYLAND

Incest; bigamy.

MASSACHUSETTS

Mental incapacity at time of marriage; under age; bigamy; incest.

MICHIGAN

Mental incapacity at time of marriage; fraud; bigamy; incest. The following grounds are valid unless the marital relationship is continued after the ground no longer exists; under age; force or duress.

MINNESOTA

Mental incapacity at time of marriage; under age; fraud; force; bigamy; incest.

71

MISSISSIPPI	Mental incapacity at time of marriage; under age; fraud; bigamy; incest; impotence at time of marriage; failure to obtain marriage license; insanity at time of marriage; wife pregnant by another at time of marriage without husband's knowledge.
MISSOURI	None. But incestuous and bigamous marriages, or those where one spouse was without mental capacity at time of marriage or a license was not obtained, are void.
MONTANA	Bigamy; incest; physical inability to perform sexual intercourse. The following grounds are valid unless the marital relationship is continued after the ground no longer exists: lack of mental capacity at time of marriage; fraud; force.
NEBRASKA	Mental illness or retardation at time of marriage; fraud; force; bigamy; impotence at time of marriage; marriage prohibited by law.
NEW HAMPSHIRE	Being under age is valid unless the marital relationship is continued after the ground no longer exists. Incestuous and bigamous marriages are void.
NEW JERSEY	Incest; bigamy; impotence at time of marriage without other spouse's knowledge. The following are valid grounds unless the marital relationship is continued after the ground no longer exists: mental incapacity at time of marriage, including that

72

caused by drugs or alcohol; under age; duress; fraud.

NEW MEXICO	Under age. Incestuous and bigamous marriages are void.
NEW YORK	Mental incapacity at time of marriage; under age; fraud; impotence; insanity (five years).
NORTH CAROLINA	Mental incapacity at time of marriage; under age; bigamy; incest; impotence.
NORTH DAKOTA	Bigamy; incest; importence at time of marriage that seems incurable. The following grounds are valid unless the marital relationship is continued after the ground no longer exists: mental incapacity at time of marriage; under age; fraud; force or duress.
OHIO	Bigamy; unconsummated marriage. The following grounds are valid unless the material relationship is continued after the ground no longer exists: mental incapacity at time of marriage; under age; fraud; force or duress. Incestuous marriages are void.
OKLAHOMA	Mental incapacity at time of marriage and being under age are valid unless the marital relationship is continued after the ground no longer exists. Incestuous and bigamous marriages are void.
OREGON	Mental incapacity at time of marriage; under age; fraud; bigamy; incest; force or duress.

PENNSYLVANIA	Mental incapacity at time of marriage; bigamy; incest.
RHODE ISLAND	None. But incestuous and bigamous marriages, or those where there was mental incapacity at the time of marriage, are void.
SOUTH CAROLINA	Mental incapacity at time of marriage; duress; bigamy; marriage not consummated.
SOUTH DAKOTA	Under age; bigamy; impotence at time of marriage which appears to be incurable. The following grounds are valid unless the marital relationship is continued after the ground no longer exists: mental incapacity; fraud; force or duress. Incestuous marriages are void.
TENNESSEE	Mental incapacity at time of marriage; under age; fraud; force or duress; bigamy; incest.
TEXAS	Under the influence of drugs or alcohol at time of marriage; under age; marriage within six months of a previous divorce. The following grounds are valid unless the marital relationship is continued after the ground no longer exists: lack of mental capacity at time of marriage; fraud; force or duress; impotence at time of marriage. Incestuous marriages are void.
UTAH	Mental incapacity at time of marriage; under age; force or duress; incest; marriage not officially solem-

nized; veneral disease; previous divorce not final.

VERMONT

Mental incapacity at time of marriage; fraud; force; impotence (one year). Being under age is valid unless the marital relationship is continued after the ground no longer exists. Incestuous and bigamous marriages are void.

VIRGINIA

Mental incapacity at time of marriage; under age; fraud; force or duress; incest; impotence; malformation preventing sexual intercourse; marriage not officially solemnized.

WASHINGTON

Under age; fraud; bigamy; incest.

WEST VIRGINIA

The following grounds are valid unless the marital relationship is continued after the ground no longer exists: mental incapacity at time of marriage; under age; fraud; force or duress; bigamy; incest; impotence; malformation preventing sexual intercourse; wife pregnant by another at time of marriage; conviction for a serious crime before marriage without spouse's knowledge; wife a prostitute before marriage without husband's knowledge; husband known to be immoral before marriage without wife's knowledge.

WISCONSIN

Mental incapacity at time of marriage; under age; fraud; force or duress; bigamy; incest; impotence; inability to perform sexual intercourse; marriage within six months of previous divorce.

75

WYOMING

Mental incapacity at time of marriage; bigamy; incest. The following are valid unless the marital relationship is continued after the ground no longer exists: under age; fraud; force or duress.

Chapter VI

EMPLOYMENT AND WOMEN

Gather together a group of women of different age groups, educational and family backgrounds and you will probably hear divergent views on "women's lib" and what its aims should be. They would all be unanimous on one point, however, and that is that one of the chief aims of the movement should be to end discriminatory practices in the hiring and compensation of male and female employees.

Traditionally, women have been given the lower paying jobs and have not been given the same advancement opportunities as men. Presumably one reason for this has been that many of the women have been married women and their pay checks supplement the earnings of their husbands. Today, with the prevalence of divorce, and with more women choosing to remain single, women are demanding equal employment opportunities and equal pay with their male counterparts. In the 1960's and 1970's, courts have begun applying the principals used in combating racial discrimination to the issue of sex discrimination in employment policies.

Two powerful weapons which women may use to combat employment discrimination are the Federal Equal Pay Act and Title VII of the 1964 Civil Rights Act. In addition there are a number of presidential orders (Executive Orders), and numerous court decisions. While the states have their own individual laws dealing with these matters of equal job opportunity and equal pay, many of them even modeled on the federal statutes, national or federal legislation is more comprehensive and carries greater weight. A woman who seeks relief for what she believes is discriminatory treatment on her job would ordinarily do so on the basis of federal guidelines and statutes, resorting to her state's laws only under very special favorable circumstances. For the purpose of this chapter, comments will be confined to the federal legislation.

Wage discrimination is prohibited by the Equal Pay Act.

Under the provisions of this Act, which is enforced by the Wage and Hours Division of the U.S. Department of Labor, a woman has two possible remedies which she might pursue if she feels that she is the subject of job discrimination. She may request an investigation of the alleged violation by the Department of Labor, which, if it finds that she has been the subject of discrimination, will initiate a law suit on her behalf to recover the unpaid wages. If she wishes she may bring her own action, and if successful, recover double the amount of unpaid wages in addition to attorney fees and court costs. At first thought, the latter alternative is more appealing, but few women could or should risk the possibility of losing the case and thereby become herself personally liable for legal fees.

The Act also provides for fines for violation of its provisions. It should also be noted that the Equal Pay Act prohibits unions from causing or allowing employers to pay unequal wages to women doing the same work as men. Unions, like employers, can be fined up to $10,000 and their officers imprisoned for six months for willful violations of the Act. But unlike employers, unions do not appear to be subject to claims for back pay through either the Department of Labor or private lawsuits.

To establish a cause of action under the Equal Pay Act, a woman must prove that her work is substantially equal to work done by her male counterpart. This means that the work requires equal skills and effort, and is performed under similar working conditions. Male workers can get higher wages than women doing the same work only on the basis of seniority, merit, quantity or quality of production differences, or any other factor not based solely on the sex of the lower-paid worker. An employer cannot comply with the Equal Pay Act simply by reducing the pay of the male worker if women are paid less for performing the same work. Compliance requires raising the pay of the women worker to equal that of their male counterparts.

In *Schulz v. Wheaton Glass Co.* the United States Supreme Court in 1970 upheld the principle that women performing work "substantially" equal to that of men should receive equal pay. *The Corning Glass Works* was required to pay a million dollars in back salaries as a result of another similar Supreme Court case.

Title VII of the Civil Rights Act, originally applied to racial discrimination cases, is an even more important federal law protecting women's employment rights. It covers, with some exceptions, private businesses with more than fifteen employees; federal, state, and local government workers; employment agencies; and labor organizations. The Equal Employment Opportunity Commission is the enforcement agency for this statute. Executive Order 11478 prohibits discrimination on the basis of sex (as well as race, religion, or national origin) in all federal agencies. Executive Order 11246 does the same thing with respect to federal contractors and sub-contractors or anyone holding a federal contract worth $10,000 or more. These Orders are enforced by the U.S. Civil Service Commission and the Office for Federal Contract Compliance respectively. Both these agencies as well as the Equal Opportunity Commission have issued Sex Discrimination Guidelines. This may be ordered directly from the EEOC. In these Guidelines the EEOC specifically bars hiring based on stereotyped characterization of the sexes; classifications labeled "men's jobs" or "women's jobs"; advertising under male or female headings; automatically terminating the employment of pregnant women; refusal to hire married women; differences in retirement age between men and women; and discrepancies between the sexes in such matters as sick leave and pay, vacation time and pay, classes given on company time, and payment while on jury duty.

Under Title VII a woman has, again, a choice of remedies. She may notify her regional EEOC office which will determine if she is covered in Title VII. If she is, she will fill out a form charging the company she works for with discrimination and giving the details of her case. The EEOC will then investigate and take the necessary steps to stop the practice if the charge is proved. On the other hand, the person who makes the charge can bring her own action.

In addition to Title VII, there are a number of Executive Orders, two of them were cited here earlier, requiring that discrimination with regard to sex be ended with respect to federal employees and those employed by holders of certain government contracts. In some instances, not only is discrimination forbidden, but affirmative action must be taken to end it. Standards have been listed to determine whether enough women are being hired. Among such standards are the number of available women within the neighborhood and the proportion employed in the particular instance. If discrimination is proved, the company involved can lose the contract.

If the basis for sex discrimination is "a bona fide occupational qualification reasonably necessary to the normal operation of that particular business or enterprise", it would not be outlawed by Title VII. Of course, the question is, *what* is a "bona fide occupational qualification provision"? The courts are still dealing with the issue. The fact that customers or clientele might show a preference for one sex over another is not an acceptable cause for discriminatory hiring practices. A case in point was the *Diaz* case where a male sought to be hired by Pan American Airlines as a flight attendant and was turned down on the ground that it was a position held only by women. The appeals court held that in spite of customer preference for female stewardesses the airline could not deny Diaz the job on the basis of his sex.

The burden of proving that sex is a "bona fide occupational qualification" is upon the employer. In one federal court case, *Rosenfeld v. Southern Pacific Railroad Co.,* the court ruled that the only two jobs in which sex is a bona fide qualification are sperm donor and wet nurse!

EEOC Guidelines list modeling, acting or jobs in the entertainment industry where sex appeal is an essential qualification as an example in which the occupation may be limited to one sex. Others would be such jobs as rest-room attendants or lingere sales clerks. Discrimination may not be practiced simply because some or most members of one sex are unable or unwilling to do the job, or because the job requires heavy physical labor, late-evening hours or because co-workers prefer one sex over another.

Title VII also bars discrimination because of child care responsibilities of employed mothers versus employed fathers.

This question was raised in *Phillips v. Martin Marietta Corporation* (1971). The suit was brought by a mother who was refused employment because she had children of pre-school age. Since men with children of the same age were hired by the Company she claimed that she suffered discrimination. The EEOC agreed with her, but the lower courts held that she was not the victim of discrimination because she was a women but because she was a woman with children of pre-school age. The Supreme Court overruled the lower court and agreed with the Title VII ruling that separate hiring practices or policies for women and men with pre-school age children are not automatically permitted. However, the decision is weak because eight of the nine justices in concurring opinions suggested that "such conflicting family obligations," if they proved to be more relevant to a woman's job performance than to a man's, *could* justify separate treatment under Title VII's bona fide occupational qualification provisions.

One of the difficult problems raised by the bona fide occupational qualification provisions of Title VII is the relationship between those provisions and a variety of state *protective* labor laws that apply only to women, such as requiring seats at work, regular rest periods, and minimum wages for female but not male employees. Some states prohibit employers from requiring or permitting women employees to work more than a designated number of hours per day or week, or to lift objects weighing more than a specified number of pounds.

The EEOC has divided protective laws into two categories: those providing women with distinct benefits, such as minimum wage laws, and others, such as hours-limitation laws, that in EEOC's opinion impose a burden upon women by depriving them of the right to earn overtime pay or by keeping them out of jobs requiring overtime work. Where state hours-limitation laws have been challenged by women workers the courts have almost unanimously invalidated those state laws as conflicting with the Title VII prohibition against sex discrimination in employment.

OCCUPATIONS BARRED TO WOMEN

ALABAMA	Mining
ALASKA	None
ARIZONA	Mining, quarrying, work on coal breakers.
ARKANSAS	Mining
CALIFORNIA	None
COLORADO	None
CONNECTICUT	None
DISTRICT OF COLUMBIA	None
FLORIDA	None
GEORGIA	None
HAWAII	None
IDAHO	None
ILLINOIS	Manual labor in mines. Local communities have authority to prohibit any woman who is not herself a liquor licensee or the wife of a licensee from drawing, pouring, or mixing alcoholic beverages as an employee of the establishment.
INDIANA	Mining
IOWA	None
KANSAS	None
KENTUCKY	May work only as waitresses, cashiers, or ushers in connection with the sale

of alcoholic beverages in taverns, bars, restaurants, and other such establishments.

LOUISIANA	None
MAINE	None
MARYLAND	None
MASSACHUSETTS	None
MICHIGAN	Any job that is disproportionate to a women's strength or which is located in a place detrimental to health, morals, or potential capacity for motherhood.
MINNESOTA	Moving molds into and out from ovens in foundries.
MISSISSIPPI	None
MISSOURI	Mining, certain work around machinery.
MONTANA	None
NEBRASKA	None
NEVADA	County liquor boards have the power to prohibit women from selling or dispensing liquor.
NEW HAMPSHIRE	None
NEW JERSEY	None
NEW MEXICO	None
NEW YORK	May not work in basements of mercantile establishments unless permission is obtained from the industrial commissioner.

NORTH CAROLINA	None
NORTH DAKOTA	May not work in any job in surroundings detrimental to health or morals.
OHIO	Mining; selling, mixing, or dispensing alcoholic beverages in establishments that cater exclusively to male customers.
OKLAHOMA	May not be employed under conditions detrimental to health or morals.
OREGON	None
PENNSYLVANIA	May not be employed in any occupation that is dangerous to life or limb or injurious to health or morals.
RHODE ISLAND	None
SOUTH CAROLINA	None
SOUTH DAKOTA	None
TENNESSEE	None
TEXAS	None
UTAH	Work in smelters and mines if found by the industrial commission to be detrimental to health and safety.
VERMONT	None
VIRGINIA	None
WASHINGTON	None
WEST VIRGINIA	Director of the Department of Mines.
WISCONSIN	None
WYOMING	None

Chapter VII

CRIME AND WOMEN

Prostitution

At common law, prostitution was not a specific crime. It was dealt with originally as an ecclesiastical offense. Today it is variously defined as "the practice of a female in offering her body to an indiscriminate intercourse with men for money or its equivalent," or "common lewdness of a woman for gain." The point about such definitions of prostitution is that they make criminal the conduct of only one party, the woman.

In most states, males cannot be directly punished for patronizing a prostitute. But, if their conduct falls within the terms of certain collateral crimes such as fornication, lewdness, solicitation, or association with a prostitute, they may be indirectly dealt with by the law. Generally, however, restrictive interpretations and the decisions made by police officials and prosecuting attorneys have more often than not led to exoneration of male customers of prostitutes.

The point is that female prostitution is unlawful in all states and the "favoritism" shown to male clients is only one of the many persisting issues of unequal treatment women face in the American legal system!

Rape

Statutory rape laws can be divided into two broad categories: 1) those requiring as an element of the crime the previous chaste character of the victim; and 2) those defining statutory rape as an unlawful carnal knowing of a female below the designated age, without regard to the victim's previous chastity. Among the first group of statutes are those in the District of Columbia, Florida, Massachusetts, and Mississippi. Unlike the others, the Mississippi Code also provides that "In the trial of all/ statutory rape cases . . . it shall be *presumed* that the female was previously of chaste character, and the burden shall be upon the defendant to show that she was not . . ."

While the states are divided on whether the previous chastity of the "victim" is an essential element of the crime of statutory rape, they are agreed that it is an indespensable part of another offense which is not unrelated to the concept of statutory rape, the crime of "seduction." Here, too, with the exception of the Massachusetts statute, the male is uniformly the offender, the female the victim. The crime of seduction is generally defined in terms of a male having deceived a female to engage in sexual intercourse by means of a false promise of marriage. In contrast to the victim of statutory rape, the victim of the crime of seduction often may be any unmarried female, regardless of age. A second distinction is that all seduction statutes require the victim to have been of previous chaste character. Seduction statutes also frequently provide that the defendant's marriage to the victim before judgment on an indictment or before a jury is sworn bars further prosecution for the crime. And, apart from criminal prosecution, a civil remedy for damages for seduction is often provided for the victim or her parent.

The states are much divided as to the female's age of consent with regard to the crime of statutory rape. The age limit ranges from fourteen years in Georgia and Maine to below age twenty-one in Tennessee.

The judicial and legislative rationalization of the concept of statutory rape in terms of the young female's legal incapacity to give her consent to intercourse is like the general contractual incapacity of minors which in turn is based on the presumption that, though there is consent in fact, legal recognition should be withheld because of the minor's presumed inability to appreciate the consequences of the agreement into which she has apparently entered.

Turning to forcible rape, it should be noted that society has a great deal of ambivalence about rape. At one extreme is the attitude, "Why struggle? Lie back and enjoy it!" Recently a TV weather cast personality was fired from his celebrated job for just such a comment jokingly. At the other extreme is the reality that the laws of fourteen states provide life imprisonment or death as maximum penalties for rape. In three states, Arkansas, Mississippi, and North Carolina, these are the *only* sentences a convicted rapist may receive.

If a suspect is apprehended and the victim agrees to press charges, the trial will be subject to the rape laws of the state, and to the rules of evidence that apply in all criminal trials. In half the states, the law does not require the victim to present evidence other than her own testimony. In eleven states, other evidence is not required if her testimony is "credible." In fourteen states, additional evidence is required, chiefly medical reports of her physical and emotional state immediately after the rape.

In all states, however, the judge must instruct the jury in a rape trial-as in every trial of a person charged with a sex offense-that the victim's testimony is to be weighed very carefully, on the ground that the accusation of rape is "easy to make but difficult to prove." This usually influences a jury to be exceedingly hesitant about convicting an alleged rapist.

There are rarely witnesses to a rape. Under the circumstances, the case comes down to the creditability of the parties, the victim and the accused. The rules of evidence in criminal trials place the "burden of proof" upon the prosecution or the complaining party. Furthermore, as a protection of the accused, nothing may be said during the trial about any prior arrests he may have had for similar offenses. This is the rule in all criminal trials, not only rape trials. In almost all states, however, (except California, Florida, and Iowa) the rape victim's sex life may be explored during the trial on the theory that it might be relevant to the issue of her consent.

The definition of rape in nearly all the state statutes is "the carnal knowledge of a woman forcibly and against her will." This means that the victim was overpowered and did not consent to the sex act. At the trial a victim must prove both that her assailant used physical violence to subdue her or seriously threatened to do so *and* that she did not *want* to perform the sex act with him. Either of these requirements alone does not satisfy the law's requirement for a valid rape charge.

However, the law does not require that the victim defend herself if in so doing she risks serious injury or death. A woman unconscious or under the influence of alcohol or drugs is incapable of resisting and therefore consent is not implied in such situations. Mental incapacity of a woman also removes the possibility of implied consent.

A man cannot be charged with raping his wife. This rule comes from the common law concept of husband and wife as one person, with the husband's authority being dominant.

AGE OF CONSENT FOR CHARGE OF FORCIBLE RAPE BY STATES

A male who has sexual relations with a female under the following ages may be charged with statutory rape:

ALABAMA	Under 16.
ALASKA	Under 16.
ARIZONA	Under 18.
ARKANSAS	Under 16.
CALIFORNIA	Under 18.
COLORADO	Under 16 and at least two years younger than charged male.
CONNECTICUT	Under 16 and charged male over 18.
DELAWARE	Under 18.
DISTRICT OF COLUMBIA	Under 16.
FLORIDA	Either a male or female who has sexual relations with a previously chaste unmarried member of the opposite sex who is under 18.
GEORGIA	Under 14.
HAWAII	Under 16.
IDAHO	Under 18.
ILLINOIS	A male over 17 who has sexual relations with a female under 16, unless he was mistaken as to her age or she was a prostitute or previously married.

INDIANA	Under 16.
IOWA	A male who has sexual relations with a female under 16 or a male over 25 who has sexual relations with a female under 17.
KANSAS	Under 16.
KENTUCKY	Either a male or female who has sexual relations with a member of the opposite sex who is under 18; however, if the male offender is between 17 and the 21, the female offender is between 18 and 21, or the younger person was previously unchaste, the penalty is much lighter than it would be otherwise.
LOUISIANA	ZUnder 17.
MAINE	A male over 18 who has sexual relations with a female under 16, or a male of any age who has sexual relations with a female under 14.
MARYLAND	Under 16; but if the female is over 14 and the male is under 18 the act is not criminal.
MASSACHUSETTS	Under 16.
MICHIGAN	Under 16.
MINNESOTA	Under 18.
MISSISSIPPI	Under 18 and previously chaste.
MISSOURI	Under 18.
MONTANA	Under 18.
NEBRASKA	Under 18 unless she is over 15 and previously unchaste.

90

NEVADA	Under 16.
NEW HAMPSHIRE	Under 16.
NEW JERSEY	Under 16.
NEW MEXICO	Under 16.
NEW YORK	A male over 21 who has sexual relations with a female under 17, or a male over 18 who has sexual relations with a female under 14.
NORTH CAROLINA	Under 16.
NORTH DAKOTA	Under 18.
OHIO	Under 16.
OREGON	Under 18.
PENNSYLVANIA	Under 16.
RHODE ISLAND	Under 16.
SOUTH CAROLINA	Under 16.
SOUTH DAKOTA	Under 16.
TENNESSEE	Under 18.
TEXAS	Under 17; but if female is over 14 and was previously unchaste, that is considered to be a mitigating circumstance.
UTAH	Under 18.
VERMONT	Under 16, but if both parties are under 16 they are both guilty of misdemeanor.
VIRGINIA	Under 16.
WASHINGTON	Under 18 and previously unchaste.

WEST VIRGINIA	Either a male or female over 16 who has sexual relations with a previously chaste member of the opposite sex who is under 16, or a male who has sexual relations with any female under 10. But penalties are much less severe for the older woman who seduces a boy than for an older man who seduces a girl.
WISCONSIN	Under 18.
WYOMING	Under 18.

APPENDIX A

Title VII of the Civil Rights Act of 1964[*]

SEC. 701. DEFINITIONS

For the purposes of this title—

(a) The term "person" includes one or more individuals, labor unions, partnerships, associations, corporations, legal representatives, mutual companies, joint-stock companies, trusts, unincorporated organizations, trustees in bankruptcy, or receivers.

(b) The term "employer" means a person engaged in an industry affecting commerce who has twenty-five or more employees for each working day in each of twenty or more calendar weeks in the current or preceding calendar year, and any agent of such a person, but such term does not include (1) the United States, a corporation wholly owned by the Government of the United States, an Indian tribe, or a State or political subdivision thereof, (2) a bona fide private membership club (other than a labor organization) which is exempt from taxation under section 501(c) of the Internal Revenue Code of 1954: *Provided,* That during the first year after the effective date prescribed in subsection (a) of section 716, persons having fewer than one hundred employees (and their agents) shall not be considered employers, and, during the second year after such date, persons having fewer than seventy-five employees (and their agents) shall not be considered employers, and, during the third year after such date, persons having fewer than fifty employees (and their agents) shall not be considered employers: *Provided further,* That it shall be the policy of the United States to insure equal employment opportunities for Federal employees without discrimination because of race, color, religion, sex or national origin and the President shall utilize his existing authority to effectuate this policy.

(c) The term "employment agency" means any person regularly undertaking with or without compensation to procure employees for an employer or to procure for employees opportunities to work for an employer and includes an agent of such a person; but shall not include an agency of the United States, or an agency of a State or political subdivision of a State, except that such terms shall include the United States Employment Service and the system of State and local employment services receiving Federal assistance.

(d) The term "labor organization" means a labor organization engaged in an industry affecting commerce, and any agent of such an organization, and includes any organization of any kind, any agency, or employee repre-

[*] 78 Stat. 253, 42 U.S.C. § 2000e et seq. (1964).

sentation committee, group, association, or plan so engaged in which employees participate and which exists for the purpose, in whole or in part, of dealing with employers concerning grievances, labor disputes, wages, rates of pay, hours, or other terms or conditions of employment, and any conference, general committee, joint or system board, or joint council so engaged which is subordinate to a national or international labor organization.

(e) A labor organization shall be deemed to be engaged in an industry affecting commerce if (1) it maintains or operates a hiring hall or hiring office which procures employees for an employer or procures for employees opportunities to work for an employer, or (2) the number of its members (or, where it is a labor organization composed of other labor organizations or their representatives, if the aggregate number of the members of such other labor organization) is (A) one hundred or more during the first year after the effective date prescribed in subsection (a) of section 716, (B) seventy-five or more during the second year after such date or fifty or more during the third year, or (C) twenty-five or more thereafter, and such labor organization—

(1) is the certified representative of employees under the provisions of the National Labor Relations Act, as amended, or the Railway Labor Act, as amended;

(2) although not certified, is a national or international labor organization or a local labor organization recognized or acting as the representative of employees of an employer or employers engaged in an industry affecting commerce; or

(3) has chartered a local labor organization or subsidiary body which is representing or actively seeking to represent employees of employers within the meaning of paragraph (1) or (2); or

(4) has been chartered by a labor organization representing or actively seeking to represent employees within the meaning of paragraph (1) or (2) as the local or subordinate body through which such employees may enjoy membership or become affiliated with such labor organization; or

(5) is a conference, general committee, joint or system board, or joint council subordinate to a national or international labor organization, which includes a labor organization engaged in an industry affecting commerce within the meaning of any of the preceding paragraphs of this subsection.

(f) The term "employee" means an individual employed by an employer.

(g) The term "commerce" means trade, traffic, commerce, transportation, transmission, or communication among the several States; or between a State and any place outside thereof; or within the District of Columbia, or a possession of the United States; or between points in the same State but through a point outside thereof.

(h) The term "industry affecting commerce" means any activity, business, or industry in commerce or in which a labor dispute would hinder or obstruct commerce or the free flow of commerce and includes any activity or industry "affecting commerce" within the meaning of the Labor-Management Reporting and Disclosure Act of 1959.

(i) The term "state" includes a State of the United States, the District of Columbia, Puerto Rico, the Virgin Islands, American Samoa, Guam, Wake Island, the Canal Zone, and Outer Continental Shelf lands defined in the Outer Continental Shelf Lands Act.

SEC. 702. EXEMPTION

This title shall not apply to an employer with respect to the employment of aliens outside any State, or to a religious corporation, association, or society with respect to the employment of individuals of a particular religion to perform work connected with the carrying on by such corporation, association, or society of its religious activities or to an educational institution with respect to the employment of individuals to perform work connected wth the educational activities of such institution.

SEC. 703. DISCRIMINATION BECAUSE OF RACE, COLOR, RELIGION, SEX, OR NATIONAL ORIGIN

(a) It shall be an unlawful employment practice for an employer—

(1) to fail or refuse to hire or to discharge any individual, or otherwise to discriminate against any individual with respect to his compensation, terms, conditions, or privileges of employment, because of such individual's race, color, religion, sex, or national origin; or

(2) to limit, segregate, or classify his employees in any way which would deprive or tend to deprive any individual of employment opportunities or otherwise adversely affect his status as an employee, because of such individual's race, color, religion, sex, or national origin.

(b) It shall be an unlawful employment practice for an employment agency to fail or refuse to refer for employment, or otherwise to discriminate against, any individual because of his race, color, religion, sex, or national origin, or to classify or refer for employment any individual on the basis of his race, color, religion, sex, or national origin.

(c) It shall be an unlawful employment practice for a labor organization—

(1) to exclude or to expel from its membership, or otherwise to discriminate against, any individual because of his race, color, religion, sex, or national origin;

(2) to limit, segregate, or classify its membership, or to classify or fail or

refuse to refer for employment any individual, in any way which would deprive or tend to deprive any individual of employment opportunities, or would limit such employment opportunities or otherwise adversely affect his status as an employee or as an applicant for employment, because of such individual's race, color, religion, sex, or national origin; or

(3) to cause or attempt to cause an employer to discriminate against an individual in violation of this section.

(d) It shall be an unlawful employment practice for any employer, labor organization, or joint labor-management committee controlling apprenticeship or other training or retraining, including on-the-job training programs to discriminate against any individual because of his race, color, religion, sex, or national origin in admission to, or employment in, any program established to provide apprenticeship or other training.

(e) Notwithstanding any other provision of this title, (1) it shall not be an unlawful employment practice for an employer to hire and employ employees, for an employment agency to classify, or refer for employment any individual, for a labor organization to classify its membership or to classify or refer for employment any individual, or for an employer, labor organization, or joint labor-management committee controlling apprenticeship or other training or retraining programs to admit or employ any individual in any such program, on the basis of his religion, sex, or national origin in those certain instances where religion, sex, or national origin is a bona fide occupational qualification reasonably necessary to the normal operation of that particular business or enterprise, and (2) it shall not be an unlawful employment practice for a school, college, university, or other educational institution or institution of learning to hire and employ employees of a particular religion if such school, college, university, or other educational institution or institution of learning is, in whole or in substantial part, owned, supported, controlled, or managed by a particular religion or by a particular religious corporation, association, or society, or if the curriculum of such school, college, university, or other educational institution or institution of learning is directed toward the propagation of a particular religion.

(f) As used in this title, the phrase "unlawful employment practice" shall not be deemed to include any action or measure taken by an employer, labor organization, joint labor-management committee, or employment agency with respect to an individual who is a member of the Communist Party of the United States or of any other organization required to register as a Communist-action or Communist-front organization by final order of the Subversive Activities Control Board pursuant to the Subversive Activities Control Act of 1950.

(g) Notwithstanding any other provision of this title, it shall not be an unlawful employment practice for an employer to fail or refuse to hire and employ any individual for any position, for an employer to discharge any individual from any position, or for an employment agency to fail or refuse to refer any individual for employment in any position, or for a labor organization to fail or refuse to refer any individual for employment in any position, if—

(1) the occupancy of such position, or access to the premises in or upon which any part of the duties of such position is performed or is to be performed, is subject to any requirement imposed in the interest of the national security of the United States under any security program in effect pursuant to or administered under any statute of the United States or any Executive order of the President; and

(2) such individual has not fulfilled or has ceased to fulfill that requirement.

(h) Notwithstanding any other provision of this title, it shall not be an unlawful employment practice for an employer to apply different standards of compensation, or different terms, conditions, or privileges of employment pursuant to a bona fide seniority or merit system, or a system which measures earnings by quantity or quality of production or to employees who work in different locations, provided that such differences are not the result of an intention to discriminate because of race, color, religion, sex, or national origin, nor shall it be an unlawful employment practice for an employer to give and to act upon the results of any professionally developed ability test provided that such test, its administration or action upon the results is not designed, intended or used to discriminate because of race, color, religion, sex or national origin. It shall not be an unlawful employment practice under this title for any employer to differentiate upon the basis of sex in determining the amount of the wages or compensation paid or to be paid to employees of such employer if such differentiation is authorized by the provisions of section 6(d) of the Fair Labor Standards Act of 1938 as amended (29 U.S.C. 206(d)).

(i) Nothing contained in this title shall apply to any business or enterprise on or near an Indian reservation with respect to any publicly announced employment practice of such business or enterprise under which a preferential treatment is given to any individual because he is an Indian living on or near a reservation.

(j) Nothing contained in this title shall be interpreted to require any employer, employment agency, labor organization, or joint labor-management committee subject to this title to grant preferential treatment to any individual or to any group because of the race, color, religion, sex, or national origin of such individual or group on account of an imbalance which may exist with respect to the total number or percentage of persons of any race, color, religion, sex, or national origin employed by any employer, referred or classified for employment by any employment agency

97

or labor organization, admitted to membership or classified by any labor organization, or admitted to, or employed in, any apprenticeship or other training program, in comparison with the total number or percentage of persons of such race, color, religion, sex, or national origin in any community, State, section, or other area, or in the available work force in any community, State, section, or other area.

SEC. 704. OTHER UNLAWFUL EMPLOYMENT PRACTICES

(a) It shall be an unlawful employment practice for an employer to discriminate against any of his employees or applicants for employment, for an employment agency to discriminate against any individual, or for a labor organization to discriminate against any member thereof or applicant for membership, because he has opposed any practice made an unlawful employment practice by this title, or because he has made a charge, testified, assisted, or participated in any manner in an investigation, proceeding, or hearing under this title.

(b) It shall be an unlawful employment practice for an employer, labor organization, or employment agency to print or publish or cause to be printed or published any notice or advertisement relating to employment by such an employer or membership in or any classification or referral for employment by such a labor organization, or relating to any classification or referral for employment by such an employment agency, indicating any preference, limitation, specification, or discrimination, based on race, color, religion, sex, or national origin, except that such a notice or advertisement may indicate a preference, limitation, specification, or discrimination based on religion, sex, or national origin when religion, sex, or national origin is a bona fide occupational qualification for employment.

SEC. 705. EQUAL EMPLOYMENT OPPORTUNITY COMMISSION

(a) There is hereby created a Commission to be known as the Equal Employment Opportunity Commission, which shall be composed of five members, not more than three of whom shall be members of the same political party, who shall be appointed by the President by and with the advice and consent of the Senate. One of the original members shall be appointed for a term of one year, one for a term of two years, one for a term of three years, one for a term of four years, and one for a term of five years, beginning from the date of enactment of this title, but their successors shall be appointed for terms of five years each, except that any individual chosen to fill a vacancy shall be appointed only for the unexpired term of the member whom he shall succeed. The President shall designate one member to serve as Chairman of the Commission, and one member to serve as Vice Chairman. The Chairman shall be responsible on behalf of the Commission for the administrative operations of the Commission, and shall appoint, in accordance with the civil service laws, such officers, agents, attorneys, and employees as it deems necessary to assist it in the performance of its functions and to fix their compensation in accordance with the Classification Act of 1949, as amended. The Vice Chairman shall act as Chairman in the absence or disability of the Chairman or in the event of a vacancy in that office.

(b) A vacancy in the Commission shall not impair the right of the remaining members to exercise all the powers of the Commission and three members thereof shall constitute a quorum.

(c) The Commission shall have an official seal which shall be judicially noticed.

(d) The Commission shall at the close of each fiscal year report to the Congress and to the President concerning the action it has taken; the names, salaries, and duties of all individuals in its employ and the moneys it has disbursed; and shall make such further reports on the cause of and means of eliminating discrimination and such recommendations for further legislation as may appear desirable.

(e) The Federal Executive Pay Act of 1956, as amended (5 U.S.C. 2201–2209), is further amended—

(1) by adding to section 105 thereof (5 U.S.C. 2204) the following clause: "(32) Chairman, Equal Employment Opportunity Commission"; and

(2) by adding to clause (45) of section 106(a) thereof (5 U.S.C. 2205(a)) the following: "Equal Employment Opportunity Commission (4)."

(f) The principal office of the Commission shall be in or near the District of Columbia, but it may meet or exercise any or all its powers at any other place. The Commission may establish such regional or State offices as it deems necessary to accomplish the purpose of this title.

(g) The Commission shall have power—

(1) to cooperate with and, with their consent, utilize regional, State, local, and other agencies, both public and private, and individuals;

(2) to pay to witnesses whose depositions are taken or who are summoned before the Commission or any of its agents the same witness and mileage fees as are paid to witnesses in the courts of the United States;

(3) to furnish to persons subject to this title such technical assistance as they may request to further their compliance with this title or an order issued thereunder;

(4) upon the request of (i) any employer, whose employees or some of them, or (ii) any labor organization, whose members or some of them, refuse or threaten to refuse to cooperate in effectuating the provisions of this title, to assist in such effectuation by conciliation or such other remedial action as is provided by this title;

(5) to make such technical studies as are appropriate to effectuate the purposes and policies of this title and to make the results of such studies

available to the public;

(6) to refer matters to the Attorney General with recommendations for intervention in a civil action brought by an aggrieved party under section 706, or for the institution of a civil action by the Attorney General under section 707, and to advise, consult, and assist the Attorney General on such matters.

(h) Attorneys appointed under this section may, at the direction of the Commission, appear for and represent the Commission in any case in court.

(i) The Commission shall, in any of its educational or promotional activities, cooperate with other departments and agencies in the performance of such educational and promotional activities.

(j) All officers, agents, attorneys, and employees of the Commission shall be subject to the provisions of section 9 of the Act of August 2, 1939, as amended (the Hatch Act), notwithstanding any exemption contained in such section.

SEC. 706. PREVENTION OF UNLAWFUL EMPLOYMENT PRACTICES

(a) Whenever it is charged in writing under oath by a person claiming to be aggrieved, or a written charge has been filed by a member of the Commission where he has reasonable cause to believe a violation of this title has occurred (and such charge sets forth the facts upon which it is based) that an employer, employment agency, or labor organization has engaged in an unlawful employment practice, the Commission shall furnish such employer, employment agency, or labor organization (hereinafter referred to as the "respondent") with a copy of such charge and shall make an investigation of such charge, provided that such charge shall not be made public by the Commission. If the Commission shall determine, after such investigation, that there is reasonable cause to believe that the charge is true, the Commission shall endeavor to eliminate any such alleged unlawful employment practice by informal methods of conference, conciliation, and persuasion. Nothing said or done during and as a part of such endeavors may be made public by the Commission without the written consent of the parties, or used as evidence in a subsequent proceeding. Any officer or employee of the Commission, who shall make public in any manner whatever any information in violation of this subsection shall be deemed guilty of a misdemeanor and upon conviction thereof shall be fined not more than $1,000 or imprisoned not more than one year.

(b) In the case of an alleged unlawful employment practice occurring in a State, or political subdivision of a State, which has a State or local law prohibiting the unlawful employment practice alleged and establishing or authorizing a State or local authority to grant or seek relief from such practice or to institute criminal proceedings with respect thereto upon receiving notice thereof, no charge may be filed under subsection (a) by the person aggrieved before the expiration of sixty days after proceedings have been commenced under the State or local law, unless such proceedings have been earlier terminated, provided that such sixty-day period shall be extended to one hundred and twenty days during the first year after the effective date of such State or local law. If any requirement for the commencement of such proceedings is imposed by a State or local authority other than a requirement of the filing of a written and signed statement of the facts upon which the proceeding is based, the proceeding shall be deemed to have been commenced for the purposes of this subsection at the time such statement is sent by registered mail to the appropriate State or local authority.

(c) In the case of any charge filed by a member of the Commission alleging an unlawful employment practice occurring in a State or political subdivision of a State, which has a State or local law prohibiting the practice alleged and establishing or authorizing a State or local authority to grant or seek relief from such practice or to institute criminal proceedings with respect thereto upon receiving notice thereof, the Commission shall, before taking any action with respect to such charge, notify the appropriate State or local officials and, upon request, afford them a reasonable time, but not less than sixty days (provided that such sixty-day period shall be extended to one hundred and twenty days during the first year after the effective day of such State or local law), unless a shorter period is requested, to act under such State or local law to remedy the practice alleged.

(d) A charge under subsection (a) shall be filed within ninety days after the alleged unlawful employment practice occurred, except that in the case of an unlawful employment practice with respect to which the person aggrieved has followed the procedure set out in subsection (b), such charge shall be filed by the person aggrieved within two hundred and ten days after the alleged unlawful employment practice occurred, or within thirty days after receiving notice that the State or local agency has terminated the proceedings under the State or local law, whichever is earlier, and a copy of such charge shall be filed by the Commission with the State or local agency.

(e) If within thirty days after a charge is filed with the Commission or within thirty days after expiration of any period of reference under subsection (c) (except that in either case such period may be extended to not more than sixty days upon a determination by the Commission that further efforts to secure voluntary compliance are warranted), the Commission has been unable to obtain voluntary compliance with this title, the Commission shall so notify the person aggrieved and a civil action may, within thirty days thereafter, be brought against the respondent named in the charge (1) by the person claiming to be aggrieved, or (2) if such charge was filed by a member of the Commission, by any person whom the charge alleges was aggrieved by the alleged unlawful employment practice. Upon application by the complainant and in such circumstances as the court may deem just, the court may appoint an attorney for such complainant and may authorize the commencement of the action without the payment of fees, costs, or security. Upon timely application, the court may, in its discretion, permit the Attorney General to intervene in such civil action if he certifies that the case is of general public importance. Upon request, the court may, in its discretion, stay further proceedings for not more than sixty days pending the termination of State or local proceedings described in subsection (b) or the efforts of the Commission to obtain voluntary compliance.

(f) Each United States district court and each United States court of a place subject to the jurisdiction of the United States shall have jurisdiction of actions brought under this title. Such an action may be brought in any judicial district in the State in which the unlawful employment practice is alleged to have been committed, in the judicial district in which the employment records relevant to such practice are maintained and administered, or in the judicial district in which the plaintiff would have worked but for the alleged unlawful employment practice, but if the respondent is not found within any such district, such an action may be brought within the judicial district in which the respondent has his principal office. For purposes of sections 1404 and 1406 of title 28 of the United States Code, the judicial district in which the respondent has his principal office shall in all cases be considered a district in which the action might have been brought.

(g) If the court finds that the respondent has intentionally engaged in or is intentionally engaging in an unlawful employment practice charged in the complaint, the court may enjoin the respondent from engaging in such unlawful employment practice, and order such affirmative action as may be appropriate, which may include reinstatement or hiring of employees, with or without back pay (payable by the employer, employment agency, or labor organization, as the case may be, responsible for the unlawful employment practice). Interim earnings or amounts earnable with reasonable diligence by the person or persons discriminated against shall operate to reduce the back pay otherwise allowable. No order of the court shall require the admission or reinstatement of an individual as a member of a union or the hiring, reinstatement, or promotion of an individual as an employee, or the payment to him of any back pay, if such individual was refused admission, suspended, or expelled or was refused employment or advancement or was suspended or discharged for any reason other than discrimination on account of race, color, religion, sex or national origin or in violation of section 704(a).

(h) The provisions of the Act entitled "An Act to amend the Judicial Code and to define and limit the jurisdiction of courts sitting in equity, and for other purposes," approved March 23, 1932 (29 U.S.C. 101-115), shall not apply with respect to civil actions brought under this section.

(i) In any case in which an employer, employment agency, or labor organization fails to comply with an order of a court issued in a civil action brought under subsection (e), the Commission may commence proceedings to compel compliance with such order.

(j) Any civil action brought under subsection (e) and any proceedings brought under subsection (i) shall be subject to appeal as provided in sections 1291 and 1292, title 28, United States Code.

(k) In any action or proceeding under this title the court, in its discretion, may allow the prevailing party, other than the Commission or the United States, a reasonable attorney's fee as part of the costs, and the Commission and the United States shall be liable for costs the same as a private person.

SEC. 707

(a) Whenever the Attorney General has reasonable cause to believe that any person or group of persons is engaged in a pattern or practice of resistance to the full enjoyment of any of the rights secured by this title, and that the pattern or practice is of such a nature and is intended to deny the full exercise of the rights herein described, the Attorney General may bring a civil action in the appropriate district court of the United States by filing with it a complaint (1) signed by him (or in his absence the Acting Attorney General), (2) setting forth facts pertaining to such pattern or practice, and (3) requesting such relief, including an application for a permanent or temporary injunction, restraining order or other order against the peson or persons responsible for such pattern or practice, as he deems necessary to insure the full enjoyment of the rights herein described.

(b) The district courts of the United States shall have and shall exercise jurisdiction of proceedings instituted pursuant to this section, and in any such proceeding the Attorney General may file with the clerk of such court a request that a court of three judges be convened to hear and determine the case. Such request by the Attorney General shall be accompanied by a certificate that, in his opinion, the case is of general public importance. A copy of the certificate and request for a three-judge court shall be immediately furnished by such clerk to the chief judge of the circuit (or in his absence, the presiding circuit judge of the circuit) in which the case is pending. Upon receipt of such request it shall be the duty of the chief judge of the circuit or the presiding circuit judge, as the case may be, to designate immediately three judges in such circuit, of whom at least one shall be a circuit judge and another of whom shall be a district judge of the court in which the proceeding was instituted, to hear and determine such case, and it shall be the duty of the judges so designated to assign the case for hearing at the earliest practicable date, to participate in the hearing and determination thereof, and to cause the case to be in every way expedited. An appeal from the final judgment of such court will lie to the Supreme Court.

In the event the Attorney General fails to file such a request in any such proceeding, it shall be the duty of the chief judge of the district (or in his absence, the acting chief judge) in which the case is pending immediately to designate a judge in such district to hear and determine the case. In the event that no judge in the district is available to hear and determine the case, the chief judge of the district, or the acting judge, as the case may be, shall certify this fact to the chief judge of the circuit (or in his absence, the acting chief judge) who shall then designate a district or circuit judge of the circuit to hear and determine the case.

It shall be the duty of the judge designated pursuant to this section to assign the case for hearing at the earliest practicable date and to cause the case to be in every way expedited.

Sec. 708. Effect on State Laws

Nothing in this title shall be deemed to exempt or relieve any person from any liability, duty, penalty, or punishment provided by any present or future law of any State or political subdivision of a State, other than any such law which purports to require or permit the doing of any act which would be an unlawful employment practice under this title.

Sec. 709. Investigations, Inspections, Records, State Agencies

(a) In connection with any investigation of a charge filed under section 706, the Commission or its designated representative shall at all reasonable times have access to, for the purposes of examination, and the right to copy any evidence of any person being investigated or proceeded against that relates to unlawful employment practices covered by this title and is relevant to the charge under investigation.

(b) The Commission may cooperate with State and local agencies charged with the administration of State fair employment practices laws and, with the consent of such agencies, may for the purpose of carrying out its functions and duties under this title and within the limitation of funds appropriated specifically for such purpose, utilize the services of such agencies and their employees and, notwithstanding any other provision of law, may reimburse such agencies and their employees for services rendered to assist the Commission in carrying out this title. In furtherance of such cooperative efforts, the Commission may enter into written agreements with such State or local agencies and such agreements may include provisions under which the Commission shall refrain from processing a charge in any cases or class of cases specified in such agreements and under which no person may bring a civil action under section 706 in any cases or class of cases so specified, or under which the Commission shall relieve any person or class of persons in such State or locality from requirements imposed under this section. The Commission shall rescind any such agreement whenever it determines that the agreement no longer serves the interest of effective enforcement of this title.

(c) Except as provided in subsection (d), every employer, employment agency, and labor organization subject to this title shall (1) make and keep such records relevant to the determinations of whether unlawful employment practices have been or are being committed, (2) preserve such records for such periods, and (3) make such reports therefrom, as the Commission shall prescribe by regulation or order, after public hearing, as reasonable, necessary, or appropriate for the enforcement of this title or the regulations or orders thereunder. The Commission shall, by regulation, require each employer, labor organization, and joint labor-management committee subject to this title which controls an apprenticeship or other training program to maintain such records as are reasonably necessary to carry out the purpose of this title, including, but not limited to, a list of applicants who wish to participate in such program, including the chronological order in which such applications were received, and shall furnish to the Commission, upon request, a detailed description of the manner in which persons are selected to participate in the apprenticeship or other training program. Any employer, employment agency, labor organization, or joint labor-management committee which believes that the application to it of any regulation or order issued under this section would result in undue hardship may (1) apply to the Commission for an exemption from the application of such regulation or order, or (2) bring a civil action in the United States district court for the district where such records are kept. If the Commission or the court, as the case may be, finds that the application of the regulation or order to the employer, employment agency, or labor organization in question would impose an undue hardship, the Commission or the court, as the case may be, may grant appropriate relief.

(d) The provision of subsection (c) shall not apply to any employer, employment agency, labor organization, or joint labor-management committee with respect to matters occurring in any State or political subdivision thereof which has a fair employment practice law during any period in which such employer, employment agency, labor organization, or joint labor-management committee is subject to such law, except that the Commission may require such notations on records which such employer, employment agency, labor organization, or joint labor-management committee keeps or is required to keep as are necessary because of differences in coverage or methods of enforcement between the State or local law and the provisions of this title. Where an employer is required by Executive Order 10925, issued March 6, 1961, or by any other Executive order prescribing fair employment practices for Government contractors and subcontractors, or by rules or regulations issued thereunder, to file reports relating to his employment practices with any Federal agency or committee, and he is substantially in compliance with such requirements, the Commission shall not require him to file additional reports pursuant to subsection (c) of this section.

(e) It shall be unlawful for any officer or employee of the Commission to make public in any manner whatever any information obtained by the Commission pursuant to its authority under this section prior to the institution of any proceeding under this title involving such information. Any officer or employee of the Commission who shall make public in any manner whatever any information in violation of this subsection shall be guilty of a misdemeanor and upon conviction thereof, shall be fined not more than $1,000, or imprisoned not more than one year.

SEC. 710. INVESTIGATORY POWERS

(a) For the purpose of any investigation of a charge filed under the authority contained in section 706, the Commission shall have authority to examine witnesses under oath and to require the production of documentary evidence relevant or material to the charge under investigation.

(b) If the respondent named in a charge filed under section 706 fails or refuses to comply with a demand of the Commission for permission to examine or to copy evidence in conformity with the provisions of section 709(a), or if any person required to comply with the provisions of section 709(c) or (d) fails or refuses to do so, or if any person fails or refuses to comply with a demand by the Commission to give testimony under oath, the United States district court for the district in which such person is found, resides, or transacts business, shall, upon application of the Commission, have jurisdiction to issue to such person an order requiring him to comply with the provisions of section 709(c) or (d) or to comply with the demand of the Commission, but the attendance of a witness may not be required outside the State where he is found, resides, or transacts business and the production of evidence may not be required outside the State where such evidence is kept.

(c) Within twenty days after the service upon any person charged under section 706 of a demand by the Commission for the production of documentary evidence or for permission to examine or to copy evidence in conformity with the provisions of section 709(a), such person may file in the district court of the United States for the judicial district in which he resides, is found, or transacts business, and serve upon the Commission a petition for an order of such court modifying or setting aside such demand. The time allowed for compliance with the demand in whole or in part as deemed proper and ordered by the court shall not run during the pendency of such petition in the court.

Such petition shall specify each ground upon which the petitioner relies in seeking such relief, and may be based upon any failure of such demand to comply with the provisions of this title or with the limitations generally applicable to compulsory process or upon any constitutional or other legal right or privilege of such person. No objection which is not raised by such a petition may be urged in the defense to a proceeding initiated by the Commission under subsection (b) for enforcement of such a demand unless such proceeding is commenced by the Commission prior to the expiration of the twenty-day period, or unless the court determines that the defendant could not reasonably have been aware of the availability of such ground of objection.

(d) In any proceeding brought by the Commission under subsection (b), except as provided in subsection (c) of this section, the defendant may petition the court for an order modifying or setting aside the demand of the Commission.

SEC. 711. NOTICES TO BE POSTED

(a) Every employer, employment agency, and labor organization, as the case may be, shall post and keep posted in conspicuous places upon its premises where notices to employees, applicants for employment, and members are customarily posted a notice to be prepared or approved by the Commission setting forth excerpts from or, summaries of, the pertinent provisions of this title and information pertinent to the filing of a complaint.

(b) A willful violation of this section shall be punishable by a fine of not more than $100 for each separate offense.

Sec. 712. Veterans' Preference

Nothing contained in this title shall be construed to repeal or modify any Federal, State, territorial, or local law creating special rights or preference for veterans.

Sec. 713. Rules and Regulations

(a) The Commission shall have authority from time to time to issue, amend, or rescind suitable procedural regulations to carry out the provisions of this title. Regulations issued under this section shall be in conformity with the standards and limitations of the Administrative Procedure Act.

(b) In any action or proceeding based on any alleged unlawful employment practice, no person shall be subject to any liability or punishment for or on account of (1) the commission by such person of an unlawful employment practice if he pleads and proves that the act or omission complained of was in good faith, in conformity with, and in reliance on any written interpretation or opinion of the Commission, or (2) the failure of such person to publish and file any information required by any provision of this title if he pleads and proves that he failed to publish and file such information in good faith, in conformity with the instructions of the Commission issued under this title regarding the filing of such information. Such a defense, if established, shall be a bar to the action or proceeding, notwithstanding that (A) after such act or omission, such interpretation or opinion is modified or rescinded or is determined by judicial authority to be invalid or of no legal effect, or (B) after publishing or filing the description and annual reports, such publication or filing is determined by judicial authority not to be in conformity with the requirements of this title.

Sec. 714. Forcibly Resisting the Commission or its Representatives

The provisions of section 111, title 18, United States Code, shall apply to officers, agents, and employees of the Commission in the performance of their official duties.

Sec. 715. Special Study by the Secretary of Labor

The Secretary of Labor shall make a full and complete study of the factors which might tend to result in discrimination in employment because of age and of the consequences of such discrimination on the economy and individuals affected. The Secretary of Labor shall make a report to the Congress not later than June 30, 1965, containing the results of such study and shall include in such report such recommendations for legislation to prevent arbitrary discrimination in employment because of age as he determines advisable.

Sec. 716. Effective Date

(a) This title shall become effective one year after the date of its enactment.

(b) Nothwithstanding subsection (a), sections of this title other than sections 703, 704, 706, and 707 shall become effective immediately.

(c) The President shall, as soon as feasible after the enactment of this title, convene one or more conferences for the purpose of enabling the leaders of groups whose members will be affected by this title to become familiar with the rights afforded and obligations imposed by its provisions, and for the purpose of making plans which will result in the fair and effective administration of this title when all of its provisions become effective. The President shall invite the participation in such conference or conferences of (1) the members of the President's Committee on Equal Employment Opportunity, (2) the members of the Commission on Civil Rights, (3) representatives of State and local agencies engaged in furthering equal employment opportunity, (4) representatives of private agencies engaged in furthering equal employment opportunity, and (5) representatives of employers, labor organizations, and employment agencies who will be subject to this title.

APPENDIX B

Executive Order 11246—Equal Employment Opportunity

Sec. 101. It is the policy of the Government of the United States to provide equal opportunity in Federal employment for all qualified persons, to prohibit discrimination in employment because of race, color, religion, sex or national origin, and to promote the full realization of equal employment opportunity through a positive, continuing program in each executive department and agency. The policy of equal opportunity applies to every aspect of Federal employment policy and practice.

Sec. 102. The head of each executive department and agency shall establish and maintain a positive program of equal employment opportunity for all civilian employees and applicants for employment within his jurisdiction in accordance with the policy set forth in Section 101.

Sec. 103. The Civil Service Commission shall supervise and provide leadership and guidance in the conduct of equal employment opportunity programs for the civilian employees of and applications for employment within the executive departments and agencies and shall review agency program accomplishments periodically. In order to facilitate the achievement of a model program for equal employment opportunity in the Federal service, the Commission may consult from time to time with such individuals, groups, or organizations as may be of assistance in improving the Federal program and realizing the objectives of this Part.

Sec. 104. The Civil Service Commission shall provide for the prompt, fair, and impartial consideration of all complaints of discrimination in Federal employment on the basis of race, color, religion, sex or national origin. Procedures for the consideration of complaints shall include at least one impartial review within the executive department or agency and shall provide for appeal to the Civil Service Commission.

Sec. 105. The Civil Service Commission shall issue such regulations, orders, and instructions as it deems necessary and appropriate to carry out its responsibilities under this Part, and the head of each executive department and agency shall comply with the regulations, orders, and instructions issued by the Commission under this Part.

Subpart A. Duties of the Secretary of Labor

Sec. 201. The Secretary of Labor shall be responsible for the administration of Parts II and III of this Order and shall adopt such rules and regulations and issue such orders as he deems necessary and appropriate to achieve the purposes thereof.

Subpart B. Contractor's Agreements

Sec. 202. Except in contracts exempted in accordance with Section 204 of this Order, all Government contracting agencies shall include in every Government contract hereafter entered into the following provisions:

"During the performance of this contract, the contractor agrees as follows:

"(1) The contractor will not discriminate against any employee or applicant for employment because of race, color, religion, sex or national origin. The contractor will take affirmative action to ensure that applicants are employed, and that employees are treated during employment, without regard to their race, color, religion, sex or national origin. Such action shall include, but not be limited to the following: employment, upgrading, demotion, or transfer; recruitment or recruitment advertising; layoff or termination; rates of pay or other forms of compensation; and selection for training, including apprenticeship. The contractor agrees to post in conspicuous places, available to employees and applicants for employment, notices to be provided by the contracting officer setting forth the provisions of this nondiscrimination clause.

"(2) The contractor will, in all solicitations or advertisements for employees placed by or on behalf of the contractor, state that all qualified applicants will receive consideration for employment without regard to race, color, religion, sex or national origin.

"(3) The contractor will send to each labor union or representative of workers with which he has a collective bargaining agreement or other contract or understanding, a notice, to be provided by the agency contracting officer, advising the labor union or workers' representative of the contractor's commitments under Section 202 of Executive Order No. 11246 of September 24, 1965, and shall post copies of the notice in conspicuous places available to employees and applicants for employment.

"(4) The contractor will comply with all provisions of Executive Order No. 11246 of Sept. 24, 1965, and of the rules, regulations, and relevant orders of the Secretary of Labor.

"(5) The contractor will furnish all information and reports required by Executive Order No. 11246 of September 24, 1965, and by the rules, regulations, and orders of the Secretary of Labor, or pursuant thereto, and will permit access to his books, records, and accounts by the contracting agency and the Secretary of Labor for purposes of investigation to ascertain compliance with such rules, regulations, and orders.

"(6) In the event of the contractor's noncompliance with the nondiscrimination clauses of this contract or with any of such rules, regulations, or orders, this contract may be cancelled, terminated or suspended in whole or in part and the contractor may be declared ineligible for further Government contracts in accordance with procedures authorized in Executive Order No. 11246 of Sept. 24, 1965, and such other sanctions may be imposed and remedies invoked as provided in Executive Order No. 11246 of September 24, 1965, or by rule, regulation, or order of the Secretary of Labor, or as otherwise provided by law.

"(7) The contractor will include the provisions of Paragraphs (1) through (7) in every subcontract or purchase order unless exempted by rules, regulations or orders of the Secretary of Labor issued pursuant to Section 204 of Executive Order No. 11246 of Sept. 24, 1965, so that such provisions will be binding upon each subcontractor or vendor. The contractor will take such action with respect to any subcontract or purchase order as the contracting agency may direct as a means of enforcing such provisions including sanctions for noncompliance: *Provided, however,* That in the event the contractor becomes involved in, or is threatened with, litigation with a subcontractor or vendor as a result of such direction by the contracting agency, the contractor may request the United States to enter into such litigation to protect the interests of the United States."

Sec. 203. (a) Each contractor having a contract containing the provisions prescribed in Section 203 shall file, and shall cause each of his subcontractors to file, Compliance Reports with the contracting agency or the Secretary of Labor as may be directed. Compliance Reports shall be filed within such times and shall contain such information as to the practices, policies, programs, and employment policies, programs, and employment statistics of the contractor and each subcontractor, and shall be in such form, as the Secretary of Labor may prescribe.

(b) Bidders or prospective contractors or subcontractors may be required to state whether they have participated in any previous contract subject to the provisions of this Order, or any preceding similar Executive order, and in that event to submit, on behalf of themselves and their proposed subcontractors, Compliance Reports prior to or as an initial part of their bid or negotiation of a contract.

(c) Whenever the contractor or subcontractor has a collective bargaining agreement or other contract or understanding with a labor union or an agency referring workers or providing or supervising apprenticeship or training for such workers, the Compliance Report shall include such information as to such labor union's or agency's practices and policies affecting compliance as the Secretary of Labor may prescribe: *Provided,* That to the extent such information is within the exclusive possession of a labor union or an agency referring workers or providing or supervising apprenticeship or training and such labor union or agency shall refuse to furnish such information to the contractor, the contractor shall so certify to the contracting agency as part of its Compliance Report and shall set forth what efforts he has made to obtain such information.

(d) The contracting agency or the Secretary of Labor may direct that any bidder or prospective contractor or subcontractor shall submit, as part of his Compliance Report, a statement in writing, signed by an authorized officer or agent on behalf of any labor union or any agency referring workers or providing or supervising apprenticeship or other training, with which the bidder or prospective contractor deals, with supporting information, to the effect that the signer's practices and policies do not discriminate on the grounds of race, color, religion, sex or national origin, and that the signer either will affirmatively cooperate in the implementation of the policy and provisions of this Order or that it consents and agrees that recruitment, employment, and the terms and conditions of employment under the proposed contract shall be in accordance with the purposes and provisions of the Order. In the event that the union, or the agency shall refuse to execute such a statement, the Compliance Report shall so certify and set forth what efforts have been made to secure such a statement and such additional factual material as the contracting agency or the Secretary of Labor may require.

Sec. 204. The Secretary of Labor may, when he deems that special circumstances in the national interest so require, exempt a contracting agency from the requirement of including any or all of the provisions of Section 202 of this Order in any specific contract, subcontract, or purchase order. The Secretary of Labor may, by rule or regulation, also exempt certain classes of contracts, subcontracts, or purchase orders (1) whenever work is to be or has been performed outside the United States and no recruitment of workers within the limits of the United States is involved; (2) for standard commercial supplies or raw materials; (3) involving less than specified amounts of money or specified numbers of workers; or (4) to the extent that they involve subcontracts below a specified tier. The Secretary of Labor may also provide, by rule, regulation, or order, for the exemption of facilities of a contractor which are in all respects separate and distinct from activities of the contractor related to the performance of the contract: *Provided,* That such an exemption will not interfere with or impede the effectuation of the purposes of this Order: *And provided further,* That in the absence of such an exemption all facilities shall be covered by the provisions of this Order.

Subpart C. Powers and Duties of the Secretary of Labor and the Contracting Agencies

Sec. 205. Each contracting agency shall be primarily responsible for obtaining compliance with the rules, regulations, and orders of the Secretary of Labor with respect to contracts entered into by such agency or its contractors. All contracting agencies shall comply with the rules of the Secretary of Labor in discharging their primary responsibility for securing compliance with the provisions of contracts and otherwise with the terms of this Order and of the rules, regulations, and orders of the Secretary of Labor issued pursuant to this Order. They are directed to cooperate with the Secretary of Labor and to furnish the Secretary of Labor such information and assistance as he may require in the performance of his functions under this Order. They are further directed to appoint or designate, from among the agency's personnel, compliance officers. It shall be the duty of such officers to seek compliance with the objectives of this Order by conference, conciliation, mediation, or persuasion.

Sec. 206. (a) The Secretary of Labor may investigate the employment practices of any Government contractor or subcontractor, or initiate such investigation by the appropriate contracting agency, to determine whether or not the contractual provisions specified in Section 202 of this Order have been violated. Such investigation shall be conducted in accordance with the procedures established by the Secretary of Labor and the investigating agency shall report to the Secretary of Labor any action taken or recommended.

(b) The Secretary of Labor may receive and investigate or cause to be investigated complaints by employees or prospective employees of a Government contractor or subcontractor which allege discrimination contrary to the contractual provisions specified in Section 202 of this Order. If this investigation is conducted for the Secretary of Labor by a contracting agency, that agency shall report to the Secretary what action has been taken or is recommended with regard to such complaints.

Sec. 207. The Secretary of Labor shall use his best efforts, directly and through contracting agencies, other interested Federal, State, and local agencies, contractors, and all other available instrumentalities to cause any labor union engaged in work under Government contracts or any agency referring workers or providing or supervising apprenticeship or training for or in the course of such work to cooperate in the implementation of the purposes of this Order. The Secretary of Labor shall, in appropriate cases, notify the Equal Employment Opportunity Commission, the Department of Justice, or other appropriate Federal agencies whenever it has reason to believe that the practices of any such labor organization or agency violate Title VI or Title VII of the Civil Rights Act of 1964 or other provision of Federal law.

Sec. 208. (a) The Secretary of Labor, or any agency, officer, or employee in the executive branch of the Government designated by rule, regulation, or order of the Secretary, may hold such hearings, public or private, as the Secretary may deem advisable for compliance, enforcement, or educational purposes.

(b) The Secretary of Labor may hold, or cause to be held, hearings in accordance with Subsection (a) of this Section prior to imposing, ordering, or recommending the imposition of penalties and sanctions under this Order. No order for debarment of any contractor from further Government contracts under Section 209(a) (6) shall be made without affording the contractor an opportunity for a hearing.

Subpart D. Sanctions and Penalties

Sec. 209. (a) In accordance with such rules, regulations, or orders as the Secretary of Labor may issue or adopt, the Secretary or the appropriate contracting agency may:

(1) Publish, or cause to be published, the names of contractors or unions which it has concluded have complied or have failed to comply with the provisions of this Order or of the rules, regulations, and orders of the Secretary of Labor.

(2) Recommend to the Department of Justice that, in cases in which there is substantial or material violation or the threat of substantial or material violation of the contractual provisions set forth in Section 202 of this Order, appropriate proceedings be brought to enforce those provisions, including the enjoining, within the limitations of applicable law, of organizations, individuals, or groups who prevent directly or indirectly, or seek to prevent directly or indirectly, compliance with the provisions of this Order.

(3) Recommend to the Equal Employment Opportunity Commission or the Department of Justice that appropriate proceedings be instituted under Title VII of the Civil Rights Act of 1964.

(4) Recommend to the Department of Justice that criminal proceedings be brought for the furnishing of false information to any contracting agency or to the Secretary of Labor as the case may be.

(5) Cancel, terminate, suspend, or cause to be cancelled, terminated, or suspended, any contract, or any portion or portions thereof, for failure of

the contractor or subcontractor to comply with the nondiscrimination provisions of the contract. Contracts may be cancelled, terminated, or suspended absolutely or continuance of contracts may be conditioned upon a program for future compliance approved by the contracting agency.

(6) Provide that any contracting agency shall refrain from entering into further contracts, or extensions or other modifications of existing contracts, with any noncomplying contractor, until such contractor has satisfied the Secretary of Labor that such contractor has established and will carry out personnel and employment policies in compliance with the provisions of this Order.

(b) Under rules and regulations prescribed by the Secretary of Labor, each contracting agency shall make reasonable efforts within a reasonable time limitation to secure compliance with the contract provisions of this Order by methods of conference, conciliation, mediation, and persuasion before proceedings shall be instituted under Subsection (a) (2) of this Section, or before a contract shall be cancelled or terminated in whole or in part under Subsection (a) (5) of this Section for failure of a contractor or subcontractor to comply with the contract provisions of this Order.

Sec. 210. Any contracting agency taking any action authorized by this Subpart, whether on its own motion, or as directed by the Secretary of Labor, or under the rules and regulations of the Secretary, shall promptly notify the Secretary of such action. Whenever the Secretary of Labor makes a determination under this Section, he shall promptly notify the appropriate contracting agency of the action recommended. The agency shall take such action and shall report the results thereof to the Secretary of Labor within such time as the Secretary shall specify.

Sec. 211. If the Secretary shall so direct, contracting agencies shall not enter into contracts with any bidder or prospective contractor unless the bidder or prospective contractor has satisfactorily complied with the provisions of this Order or submits a program for compliance acceptable to the Secretary of Labor or, if the Secretary so authorizes, to the contracting agency.

Sec. 212. Whenever a contracting agency cancels or terminates a contract, or whenever a contractor has been debarred from further Government contracts, under Section 209(a) (6) because of noncompliance with the contract provisions with regard to nondiscrimination, the Secretary of Labor, or the contracting agency involved, shall promptly notify the Comptroller General of the United States. Any such debarment may be rescinded by the Secretary of Labor or by the contracting agency which imposed the sanction.

Subpart E. Certificates of Merit

Sec. 213. The Secretary of Labor may provide for issuance of a United States Government Certificate of Merit to employers or labor unions, or other agencies which are or may hereafter be engaged in work under Government contracts, if the Secretary is satisfied that the personnel and employment practices of the employer, or that the personnel, training, apprenticeship, membership, grievance and representation, upgrading, and other practices and policies of the labor union or other agency conform to the purposes and provisions of this Order.

Sec. 214. Any Certificate of Merit may at any time be suspended or revoked by the Secretary of Labor if the holder thereof, in the judgment of the Secretary, has failed to comply with the provisions of this Order.

Sec. 215. The Secretary of Labor may provide for the exemption of any employer, labor union, or other agency from any reporting requirements imposed under or pursuant to this Order if such employer, labor union, or other agency has been awarded a Certificate of Merit which has not been suspended or revoked.

PART III. NON-DISCRIMINATION PROVISIONS IN FEDERALLY ASSISTED CONSTRUCTION CONTRACTS

Sec. 301. Each executive department and agency which administers a program involving Federal financial assistance shall require as a condition for the approval of any grant, contract, loan, insurance, or guarantee thereunder, which may involve a construction contract, that the applicant for Federal assistance undertake and agree to incorporate, or cause to be incorporated, into all construction contracts paid for in whole or in part with funds obtained from the Federal Government or borrowed on the credit of the Federal Government pursuant to such grant, contract, loan, insurance, or guarantee, or undertaken pursuant to any Federal program involving such grant, contract, loan, insurance, or guarantee, the provisions prescribed for Government contracts by Section 203 of this Order or such modification thereof, preserving in substance the contractor's obligations thereunder, as may be approved by the Secretary of Labor, together with such additional provisions as the Secretary deems appropriate to establish and protect the interest of the United States in the enforcement of those obligations. Each such applicant shall also undertake and agree (1) to assist and cooperate actively with the administering department or agency and the Secretary of Labor in obtaining the compliance of contractors and subcontractors with those contract provisions and with the rules, regulations, and relevant orders of the Secretary, (2) to obtain and to furnish to the administering department or agency and to the Secretary of Labor such information as they may require for the supervision of such compliance, (3) to carry out sanctions and penalties for violation of such obligations imposed upon contractors and subcontractors by the Secretary of Labor or the administering department or agency pursuant to Part II, Subpart D, of this Order, and (4) to refrain from entering into any contract to this Order, or extension or other modification of such a contract with a contractor debarred from Government contracts under Part II, Subpart D, of this Order.

Sec. 302. (a) "Construction contract" as used in this Order means any contract for the construction, rehabilitation, alteration, conversion, extension, or repair of buildings, highways, or other improvements to real property.

(b) The provisions of Part II of this Order shall apply to such construction contracts, and for purposes of such application the administering department or agency shall be considered the contracting agency referred to therein.

(c) The term "applicant" as used in this Order means an applicant for Federal assistance or, as determined by agency regulation, other program participant, with respect to whom an application for any grant, contract, loan, insurance, or guarantee is not finally acted upon prior to the effective date of this Part, and it includes such an applicant after he becomes a recipient of such Federal assistance.

Sec. 303. (a) Each administering department and agency shall be responsible for obtaining the compliance of such applicants with their undertakings under this Order. Each administering department and agency is directed to cooperate with the Secretary of Labor, and to furnish the Secretary such information and assistance as he may require in the performance of his functions under this Order.

(b) In the event an applicant fails and refuses to comply with his undertakings, the administering department or agency may take any or all of the following actions: (1) cancel, terminate, or suspend in whole or in part the agreement, contract, or other arrangement with such applicant with respect to which the failure and refusal occurred; (2) refrain from extending any further assistance to the applicant under the program with respect to which the failure or refusal occurred until satisfactory assurance of future compliance has been received from such applicant; and (3) refer the case to the Department of Justice for appropriate legal proceedings.

(c) Any action with respect to an applicant pursuant to Subsection (b) shall be taken in conformity with Section 602 of the Civil Rights Act of 1964 (and the regulations of the administering department or agency issued thereunder), to the extent applicable. In no case shall action be taken with respect to an applicant pursuant to Clause (1) or (2) of Subsection (b) without notice and opportunity for hearing before the administering department or agency.

Sec. 304. Any executive department or agency which imposes by rule, regulation, or order requirements of nondiscrimination in employment, other than requirements imposed pursuant to this Order, may delegate to the Secretary of Labor by agreement such responsibilities with respect to compliance standards, reports, and procedures as would tend to bring the administration of such requirements into conformity with the administration of requirements imposed under this Order: *Provided,* That actions to effect compliance by recipients of Federal financial assistance with requirements imposed pursuant to Title VI of the Civil Rights Act of 1964 shall be taken in conformity with the procedures and limitations prescribed in Section 602 thereof and the regulations of the administering department or agency issued thereunder.

PART IV. MISCELLANEOUS

Sec. 401. The Secretary of Labor may delegate to any officer, agency, or employee in the Executive branch of the Government, any function or duty of the Secretary under Parts II and III of this Order, except authority to promulgate rules and regulations of a general nature.

Sec. 402. The Secretary of Labor shall provide administrative support for the execution of the program known as the "Plans for Progress."

Sec. 403. (a) Executive Orders Nos. 10590 (January 19, 1955), 10722 (August 5, 1957), 10925 (March 6, 1961), 11114 (June 22, 1963), and 11162 (July 28, 1964), are hereby superseded and the President's Committee on Equal Employment Opportunity established by Executive Order No. 10925 is hereby abolished. All records and property in the custody of the Committee shall be transferred to the Civil Service Commission and the Secretary of Labor, as appropriate.

(b) Nothing in this Order shall be deemed to relieve any person of any obligation assumed or imposed under or pursuant to any Executive Order superseded by this Order. All rules, regulations, orders, instructions, designations, and other directives issued by the President's Committee on Equal Employment Opportunity and those issued by the heads of various departments or agencies under or pursuant to any of the Executive orders superseded by this Order, shall, to the extent that they are not inconsistent with this Order, remain in full force and effect unless and until revoked or superseded by appropriate authority. References in such directives to provisions of the superseded orders shall be deemed to be references to the comparable provisions of this Order.

Sec. 404. The General Services Administration shall take appropriate action to revise the standard Government contract forms to accord with the provisions of this Order and of the rules and regulations of the Secretary of Labor.

Sec. 405. This Order shall become effective thirty days after the date of this Order.

INDEX